MUCH ADO
ABOUT NOTHING

For Sam Goldwyn, Jr., and Tom Rothman, with thanks

MUCH ADO
ABOUT NOTHING

by William Shakespeare

Screenplay, Introduction, and Notes on

the Making of the Movie by

Kenneth Branagh

Photographs by Clive Coote

W.W. Norton & Company · New York · London

The text of this book is composed in Monotype News Gothic and Sabon
Composition by Shaun Webb Graphic Design, 83 Berwick Street, London W1V 3PJ
Colour printing by Coral Graphic Services Inc.
Manufacturing by The Haddon Craftsmen Inc.
Book design by Shaun Webb Graphic Design

Library of Congress Cataloging-in-Publication Data

Branagh, Kenneth.
Much Ado About Nothing: the Making of the Movie / Kenneth Branagh.
Includes screenplay based on the play by William Shakespeare.
1 Much Ado About Nothing (Motion Picture)
i Shakespeare, William 1546–1616. Much Ado About Nothing
ii Title PN1997 M793B7 1993
791 43'72–dc20 93–3330

ISBN 0-393-03568-9 (cl)
ISBN 0-393-31111-2 (pa)

W.W. Norton & Company, Inc., 500 Fifth Avenue, New York, N.Y. 10110
W.W. Norton & Company Ltd., 10 Coptic Street, London WC1A 1PU

 3 4 5 6 7 8 9 0

Contents

Introduction

Page vi

Synopsis

by Russell Jackson

Page 1

The screenplay

Page 4

The cast

Character notes by Russell Jackson

Page 85

The film

Page 97

The shoot

Page 117

Why make a new film of *Much Ado About Nothing*? In this century, Shakespeare's play has been produced as a feature film on four occasions. The first was an American silent version in 1926; an East German version was made in 1963, and two Russian films appeared in 1956 and 1973. There have also been television versions, often of notable stage productions like Franco Zeffirelli's in 1967 and Joseph Papp's in 1973. But why no modern cinema version?

Certainly the movie world's financers have always evinced suspicion about the commercial possibilities of Shakespeare on film. Yet 'popular' plays like *Romeo and Juliet* or *Hamlet* have not only worked spectacularly in film versions by Zeffirelli and Sir Laurence Olivier but have proved commercial enough to be repeated on film many times. There are sixty movie versions of *Hamlet*.

It seems odd that *Much Ado About Nothing* has not fallen into this category. Since Shakespeare wrote the play, in the mid to latter part of 1598, it has been an enduring success. The 1600 edition tells us that by then it had been 'sundrie times publikely acted.' The play was certainly a crowd pleaser and puller. The poet Leonard Digges observed,

> *Let but Beatrice*
> *And Benedick be seen, lo, in a trice*
> *The cockpit, galleries, boxes, all are full.*

The role of Dogberry was an enormous success for the first great clown of Shakespeare's company, Will Kempe. Down the centuries since, the leading roles have attracted many notable actors: David Garrick, Henry Irving, Ellen Terry, and, in our own time, John Gielgud, Peggy Ashcroft, and Maggie Smith. But does this play rest too completely on the *'kind of merry war twixt Signior Benedick and her'* [Beatrice]? And can the expression of this conflict, in puns, courtly wit, verbal conceits, translate into the medium of film? Can its identity-defining wordplay be dramatic in a screenplay?

Well, yes, I believe it can, but more than that, I believe a film of *Much Ado* allows us to see in unique focus the breadth of a play that goes much further than the celebration of one gloriously witty couple. Beatrice and Benedick are, after all, the subplot.

The challenge for a new film of *Much Ado* is not to resist Beatrice and Benedick's dominance but, through the choices made by the camera, to bring to vivid life all the other characters. To take on the play as a whole and realize fully-fleshed lives, for characters like the Friar, the Watch, and Leonato's household in a realistic background and an evocative landscape. Against this detail the Beatrice and Benedick sequences do not sit merely as star turns. Perhaps most importantly, there is room in a movie to give a different kind of space to the Claudio/Hero plot.

My first thoughts about a film version occurred in 1988. At that time I had not yet directed my first feature film (Shakespeare's *Henry V*), but I found that often after seeing a play, filmic images suggested by the play would haunt me. The 'movie' would start to run in my imagination. All the more vividly, perhaps, because at that stage I had no real idea that I would ever have the opportunity to make the movies in my mind translate to celluloid.

The opening images for this film of *Much Ado About Nothing* came to me during an actual stage performance of the play when I have to confess my concentration wandered. I was playing Benedick in a beautiful production directed by Dame Judi Dench on a U.K. tour. One night during Balthasar's song 'Sigh No More, Ladies,' the title sequence of this film played over and over in my mind: heat haze and dust, grapes and horseflesh, and a nod to *The Magnificent Seven*. The men's sexy arrival, the atmosphere of rural Messina, the vigour and sensuality of the women, possessed me in the weeks, months, and years that followed. This long-term marination process was vital in convincing me that a film of *Much Ado* could work. Opening the story for the cinema, I thought, should not mean drowning the words and characters in endless vistas and 'production value.' Yet the play seemed to beg to live outside, in a vivid, lush countryside. Making the right stylistic connection between word and picture took me four years and three more films to achieve.

During that time I'd become even more convinced of the necessity of doing the film. There were many reasons. The experience of putting Shakespeare on screen as in *Henry V* had been an extraordinary lesson. A continuous and consistent stream of mail from around the world confirmed the huge appetite for affordable, truly modern accounts of this man's work. Our *Henry V* had encouraged many (including vast numbers of children) to develop their own, healthily critical view of Shakespeare. This, in a medium with which they were already familiar and to which they had far greater access than to the theatre.

Many of those who wrote had enjoyed the apparent 'naturalness' of the acting (which I think is depressing testament to the usual expectation of incomprehensible booming and fruity-voiced declamation). My continued desire in *Much Ado* was for an absolute clarity that would enable a modern audience to respond to Shakespeare on film, in the same way that they would respond to any other movie. Our concern was to do this without losing his unique poetry.

Ironically, three-quarters of *Much Ado* is in prose. But if there is such a thing as 'poetic prose,' then Shakespeare achieves it in this play. It has a double effect. It can give us the poetic melancholy of Beatrice's '*No, sure, my lord, my mother cried. But then there was a star danced and under that was I born.*' But at the same time much of the dialogue has a realistic, conversational tone that renders it most easy on the ear.

The prose wooing scene between Henry and Katherine at the end of *Henry V* prompted many viewers to say that we had made up the dialogue. When we played *Much Ado* in the theatre, this charge was made regularly by backstage visitors. The accusation was not true, but it did say much about the realistic quality of the play. It hinted also at the style our Renaissance Theatre Company had begun to develop, a style on which the acting in the films of *Henry V* and *Much Ado* would be based.

During our theatre company's short life we have tackled several of Shakespeare's comedies. In each case the productions have, in broad terms, sought out the particular quality that has spoken most loudly to the directors and actors involved. In the case of *Twelfth Night* it was the bitter melancholy of the piece that attracted us. That sense of irony and regret, shot through the comedy, made our rendition closer to Chekhov than is perhaps usual. With *As You Like It*, the sheer joy of its pastoral lyricism was emphasised; the acting was playful and delicate. *Much Ado About Nothing* seemed much more robust in tone, rougher and sexier than our Forest of Arden in *As You Like It*. Its hot-tempered Italianate qualities distinguish it from the more obvious 'Englishness' of the other plays.

But in the case of each of these stage productions, our intent was to disarm the audience with the 'reality' of the playing. Our troupe was young and often inexperienced. But the actors were cast for their talent and for the freshness they brought to the roles. Like me, many of the actors were coming to the plays for the first time. They were relatively free of actory mannerisms and the baggage of strutting and bellowing that accompanies the least effective Shakespearean performances.

Ours was a style that wished to be in tune with our audience. We were touring around the United Kingdom and Ireland to places and audiences that were also relatively unfamiliar with these plays. Our great joy was to set and tell the story with the utmost clarity and simplicity and let the particular directorial inflexion, or interpretation, be seen through the characterisations. In effect, we assumed that no one had seen the play before. We wanted audiences to react to the story as if it were in the here and now and important to them. We did not want them to feel they were in some cultural church.

We made the same attempt in film. The goal was utter reality of characterisation. Shakespeare accomplishes this as a matter of course. The difficulty for actors lies in not putting things in between themselves and this reality – a funny voice, a walk, an unconscious treatment of the character that suggests he or she is from another planet. The film medium resists such artifice completely. The camera in a film of *Much Ado* would ruthlessly sniff out any artificial 'witty' acting – flutey voiced young gallants with false laughs and thighs made for slapping.

Indeed, I required absolutely the opposite. This film would be based on character. In the absence of an eventful plot (the irony of the title is not lost on us), it is the detail of humanity amongst the participants that helps make *Much Ado* one of Shakespeare's most accessible works.

The film presented a rare opportunity to utilise the skills of marvellous film actors who would embrace this naturalistic challenge. I was determined, however, not to cast only British actors. I wanted a combination of elements that would exploit the novelty of doing Shakespeare on film. Unlike the plays performed on our theatrical tours, this film would be seen mostly by people coming fresh to Shakespeare in movie form. I wanted something of that atmosphere on the set.

In crude terms, the challenge was to find experienced Shakespearean actors who were unpracticed on screen and team them with highly experienced film actors who were much less familiar with Shakespeare. Different accents, different looks. An excitement borne out of complementary styles and approaches would produce a Shakespeare film that belonged to the world. As a longtime admirer of American screen acting, I naturally wished to include some U.S. actors. In place of events, much of the action in this piece comes from the characters' emotional volatility. The best American film acting has always had this emotional fearlessness.

Making this work called for the appropriate casting chemistry and a formal rehearsal period prior to shooting. The casting of the British actors was relatively straightforward. Richard Briers, Emma Thompson, Brian Blessed et al., had spent much of the previous five years working with Renaissance and being part of the developing style I've tried to describe. I had no set number of American actors that I tried to cast. Indeed, I was also interested in one or two Italian and French actors. My aim was to be as international as possible. In the end the choices became simple. I asked film actors whom I admired and whose career choices had been adventurous enough to suggest they would not be intimidated. In all cases I explained that I did not want artificial 'Shakespeare voices,' that they must perform in their own accents, and that they must be prepared to study the text technically, as well as carry out their absolute obligation to be truthful.

The rehearsal process was designed to accommodate these tasks. One of the people in attendance was Russell Jackson of the Shakespeare Institute in Stratford-Upon-Avon. His special responsibility was to make each actor aware of when a character was speaking in verse and when in prose, and to make him aware, in either case, of the rhythm of the text. Russell pointed out places where particular words were repeated for effect, places where a character's vocabulary gave a clue to personality, and devices such as onomatopoeia and alliteration – in short, any appreciation of where the music of the language breathed, stopped, paused, etc. All this to ensure that the spontaneity, freshness, and naturalism that we were after were achieved with a bedrock of structural understanding. Realistic Shakespearean acting on film or on stage cannot be achieved fully without this understanding. Whatever the effect we strive for, we must remember at all times that we are speaking the words of a great dramatic poet. His poetry, of whatever kind, must be observed.

Also present at rehearsal was Hugh Cruttwell, former director and principal of the Royal Academy of Dramatic Art in London. Hugh had two roles on the production. One was to ensure that in the midst of other responsibilities my performance as Benedick did not suffer. He was my other eye. A secondary function was to be a help to the actors in establishing their characters. These were arrived at in a variety of ways. I had solo sessions with each of the actors, and we held group

discussions/improvisation sessions to explore the background
to our world.

How long had the soldiers been away? What kind of war had it been?
How violent? Which of our men had been killers? How often had they
visited Leonato prior to this? How well did they all know one another?
How old were they? How long did these soldiers expect to live?

And then, of course, we probed the detail of the relationships. This
filling in of the 'back story' for each of the characters is one of the most
necessary and interesting elements in preparing a characterisation,
particularly for the screen. The audience won't know specifically my offscreen history for Benedick – his upbringing, his family, his likes and
dislikes – but I hope that with this history firmly in my mind, they will at
least intuit part of it, feel a depth to the character beyond what he says
and does.

With Benedick and Beatrice, a shared understanding between the
actors of their mutual history was essential. They are both described as
'merry.' Leonato says of Beatrice,

> There's little of the melancholy element in her, my lord;
> she is never sad but when she sleeps, and not ever sad then;
> for I have heard my daughter say she hath often dreamt of
> unhappiness and waked herself with laughing.

Yet many productions interestingly choose to mine that part of Beatrice
and Benedick's history which, if not tinged by melancholy, is at least
spoken of with some regret by Beatrice, who when charged with losing
the heart of Benedick replies,

> Indeed, my lord, he lent it me awhile, and I gave
> him use for it, a double heart for his single one.
> Marry, once before he won it of me with false dice,
> therefore your grace may well say I have lost it.

Emma Thompson and I both wanted to suggest former lovers who had
been genuinely hurt by their first encounter, which perhaps occurred at
the tender age of Hero and Claudio in the play. (For our purposes we
deliberately made the younger lovers around twenty years of age and
Beatrice and Benedick a significant ten years or so older.) In our version,
both characters are at that point where they might well develop into
confirmed spinster and bachelor. Both are staunchly anti-marriage and
very resistant to the way in which that institution mutes the personalities
of such as themselves. But the foundation of the performance was the
idea of two people who had broken each other's hearts and who had
developed personalities that attempted to prevent the same thing ever
happening again. Their wit, irony, and apparent lack of feeling covers
only superficially two of the most romantic, generous, and emotional of
Shakespeare's characters.

This emotional volatility was a key to the whole film. We wished to involve the audience's hearts as well as their minds and their laughter muscles.

Robert Sean Leonard (Claudio), Denzel Washington (Don Pedro), and Keanu Reeves (Don John) all wished to stress the full-blooded nature of their respective characters. These men are soldiers for whom time spent away from war is precious. Love is *seized*. The instantaneousness of Claudio's love for Hero, its intensity, is not unusual amongst men for whom death is an equal reality. Hence the swiftness and the delight with which Don Pedro takes up his young charge's case. There is a zeal to the Don's playfulness that is almost too intense. We enjoy his fun but at the same time cannot fail to be worryingly aware of Don John's malevolent, equally passionate presence. The atmosphere in the early part of the play recalls Juliet's reservations before her fateful date with Romeo.

> *I have no joy of this contract tonight.*
> *It is too rash, too unadvised, too sudden;*
> *Too like the lightning, which doth cease to be*
> *Ere one can say it lightens.*

There is much rashness in *Much Ado*. The speed of the plot allows people to abandon rationality in the face of often incredible events.

As in much of Shakespeare, a strong suspension of disbelief is necessary when it comes to the plot of *Much Ado*. Lewis Carroll is very funny about it in a letter to Ellen Terry:

> *My difficulty is this: Why in the world did not Hero (or at any rate Beatrice when speaking on her behalf) prove an 'alibi', in answer to the charge? It seems certain she did not sleep in her own room that night: for how could Margaret venture to open the window and talk from it, with her mistress asleep in the room? It would be sure to wake her. Besides, Borachio says, after promising that Margaret shall speak with him out of Hero's chamber-window, 'I will so fashion the matter that Hero shall absent.' (How he could possibly manage any such thing is another difficulty: but I pass over that.)*
>
> *Well, then, granting that Hero slept in some other room that night, why didn't she say so? When Claudio asks her, 'What man was he talked with you yesterday out at your window betwixt twelve and one?' why doesn't she reply, 'I talked with no man at that hour, my lord: Nor was I in my chamber yesternight, but in another, far from it remote.' And this she could prove by the evidence of the housemaid, who must have known that she had occupied another room that night.*
>
> *But even if Hero might be supposed to be so distracted as not to remember where she had slept the night before, or even whether she had slept anywhere,*

surely Beatrice has her wits about her? And when an
arrangement was made, by which she was to lose, for
that one night, her twelve-months' bedfellow, is it
conceivable that she didn't know where Hero passed the
night? Why didn't she reply

But, good my lord, sweet Hero slept not there:
She had another chamber for the nonce.
'Twas sure some counterfeit that did present
Her person at the window, aped her voice,
Her mien, her manners, and hath thus deceived
My good lord Pedro and this company.

That this whole story should be resolved by the comic intervention of a ludicrous constable lends to *Much Ado* a warmly bizarre quality that does much to amend the ugliness inherent in the wedding scene and in Claudio's behaviour afterwards. Michael Keaton and I were agreed that Dogberry should be not only a verbal but a physical malaprop. I suspect I am not alone in finding the character's play on words less funny today than the character himself – instantly recognisable, a universal type, beautifully pompous, and, in our version, dangerous too. A modern cinema audience, ready to scream at Dogberry for his inability to inform Leonato of the plot against Hero in time, needed to know exactly why he does not.

In our version this is quite clear. Dogberry combines an awe and envy of authority that renders him barely able to speak in the presence of someone like Leonato or Don Pedro. When he does speak, it is with the confused confidence of the psychopath. In our film Dogberry and Verges are charismatically, indomitably mad. The Watch, who are featured throughout the film, are awed and frightened by him. This element of danger allows the audience to feel uncertain about whether the plot will ever truly resolve itself. That unbalancing of expectations, a useful doubt about what would happen next, was something we actively sought.

For a film of Shakespeare should have no empty moments. As in *Henry V*, where we featured the faces of an otherwise anonymous English army that became known to us, in *Much Ado* Leonato's household are present throughout. Their reaction at the wedding becomes that much more powerful, their joy at the end that much more intense. In the theatre when there is a palpable sense of 'company,' the audience is aware of it in a very satisfying way. Our rehearsals did as much to promote this sense of one Messinian community as possible.

On the production side we made sure that the costumes and period setting did everything they could to release the audience's imagination. We consciously avoided setting this version in a specific time but instead went for a look that worked within itself, where clothes, props, architecture, all belonged to the same world. This imaginary world could have existed almost anytime between 1700 and 1900. It was distant enough to allow the language to work without the clash of period anachronisms and for a certain fairy tale quality to emerge. This fairy tale idea seemed to spring naturally out of the countryside in which we were working. We were in Tuscany, central Italy, a magical landscape of vines and olives that seems untouched by much of modern life. Lusher and more verdant than Sicily (Shakespeare's setting), it allowed us to create a visual idyll in which this cautionary tale might be told.

If there is a single moral to be taken from this story, it is one that I chose to find in the song that begins the film.

> *Sigh no more, ladies, sigh no more.*
> *Men were deceivers ever,*
> *One foot in sea and one on shore,*
> *To one thing constant never.*
> *Then sigh not so, but let them go,*
> *And be you blithe and bonny,*
> *Converting all your sounds of woe*
> *Into Hey nonny, nonny.*
>
> *Sing no more ditties, sing no more,*
> *Of dumps so dull and heavy;*
> *The fraud of men was ever so,*
> *Since summer first was leafy.*
> *Then sigh not so, but let them go,*
> *And be you blithe and bonny,*
> *Converting all your sounds of woe*
> *Into Hey nonny, nonny.*

We hear the song three times in the film. Once in Beatrice's wry, ironic voice at the beginning, again at the centre of the film, in an idealised garden setting where it appeals to Claudio's high romanticism, and finally at the end where it becomes a hard-won confirmation of a certain reality in the relationships between men and women. The idea of seeing the words and hearing them spoken right at the beginning of the film was a determined attempt to show how they could be dramatic in themselves. It allows the audience to 'tune in' to the new language they are about to experience and to realise (I hope) that they will easily understand the simplicity, gravity, and beauty of the song lyrics.

Purists may be offended; the play does not begin in this way. But this decision does raise the issue of what one means exactly by 'adapting' Shakespeare. I think that in film terms, it means giving a strong sense of the interpretive line. In the comedies this is crucial. They must be inflected. They do not lay themselves out with the same strong narrative, historical frame that the history plays do. The very titles themselves invite us to be bold: *Twelfth Night, or What You Will. As You Like It.*

In the case of this screenplay (whose planned mise-en-scène was adhered to far more strictly than in any other film on which I've worked) there is a great deal of description. Particularly at the beginning much is made of atmosphere and characters' states of mind. This seemed necessary for a play like *Much Ado*, which has been set in every conceivable period and country, with young, old, and middle-aged casting of every permutation. We did cut lines and occasionally scenes where the plot (such as it is) was not advanced. We did transpose some scenes in order to create a movie pace (quite different from that of the theatre).

For example, in the very first scene, it seemed to me important to get to the men's arrival as soon as possible. We would shortly see them riding to Leonato's. Excessive description of what Benedick and Claudio were like therefore seemed unnecessary.

The Beatrice and Benedick gulling scenes were trimmed in such a way as to make one big scene of continuous action in the same garden. We wanted to lose any sense of the formal ending of one scene and beginning of another as in the play. This helped the believability of the two characters' falling for each other so swiftly. It also took acting pressure off the women in the second of the scenes. In the theatre this is often a difficult scene, as it has to in some way 'top' the boys' gulling scene. This is impossible, as the second scene's tone is quite different, less obviously funny.

The deception of Claudio was most important in this screen adaptation. In theatrical versions this character is often dismissed for his gullibility. Hero's alleged infidelity (her 'talking' to a man at a window) is described as happening offstage. It seemed that if we saw this occur on screen, it would add a new dimension to our understanding of Claudio. This proof of her disloyalty is one of a number of crucial events that take place on the night before the wedding. To extract maximum drama (and comedy) from this night, we made some transpositions. Don John's scene with Borachio where they plot the deception was moved from before the gulling scenes (as in the play) to afterwards, as if at the beginning of this one terrible night. This had the side effect of distributing Don John's appearances more evenly and satisfyingly through the film. We broke up the first Watch scene, bringing Dogberry into the story earlier and cutting after his first exit, allowing the dastardly events of this night to occur with greater film logic. Time passes while the deception occurs, and then we come back to the sleeping constabulary ready to arrest Borachio and Conrade.

In the Dogberry scenes we cut the unfunniest lines. (I realise this is an entirely subjective issue, but having played one of the great unfunny Shakespearean clowns – Touchstone in *As You Like It* – I speak from bitter experience.) The wedding morning scene between the women, where Beatrice's love-induced 'cold' is made much fun of by Margaret, was shot. But although beautifully acted it was cut on the grounds that the dramatic way in which the previous nighttime sequence had played made the audience alive with expectation for the events of the wedding itself. This scene with the girls seemed finally to frustrate.

Elsewhere the cuts mainly involved the repetition of plot. In the play, characters constantly restate the current shape of events and repeat what's just happened and what's about to happen. But nothing 'difficult' was changed. No words were altered for easier understanding. The adaptation was at the service of our attempt to find an essence in the piece, to find the spirit of the play itself.

This brings me back to my first question. Why film *Much Ado About Nothing*? And why now?

When I was training to be an actor at the Royal Academy of Dramatic Art, this question of *why?* was something Hugh Cruttwell constantly urged me to consider. The *how* of creating a piece of art always comes second. It's the *why* that will get you to the truth of a character. Why does Benedick love Beatrice? Not how – that's easy. Answering *why* always takes forever when creating a character, but it's a necessary journey. An actor has to apply the same question to himself when creating a film, or when performing a play. With the luxury of a degree of choice, a proper answer has to go beyond 'So I can earn a living' or 'It's a lovely part' or 'I like Italy.' One has to ask why one is communicating this particular story at this particular time.

So, once again, why *Much Ado About Nothing*? Well, for me, because it speaks loudly and gloriously about love, one of humankind's permanent obsessions. The cruelty of it, the joy of it. The question of tolerance in love and the danger of judging others. The cost of the ambiguous maturity that people like Hero and Claudio enjoy. The loss of innocence; the power of lust; our obsession with sex and the flesh. The persistent presence of sheer, unmotivated evil in the world as provided by the Iago prototype Don John.

In short, the play presents a whole series of emotional and spiritual challenges that we – young, old, male, female – continue to face when we love. And all throughout this comic debate about everything and nothing, there is life-giving, wisdom-bearing humour and warmth. The piece is harsh and cruel as people can be. It is generous and kind as they can also be. It is uplifting but never sentimental. It '*holds the mirror up to nature*' and allows us inside its wonderful warts-and-all world of human nature, to understand and perhaps even to forgive ourselves for some of our oft-repeated follies.

That's why I interpreted *Much Ado About Nothing* on film in 1993. The attempt to achieve all this and any degree of success is due to a massive team effort. My thanks to producers, production team, cast, and crew for making it all possible.

Synopsis

Leonato, a wealthy and respected citizen of Messina, is picnicking with his family: his brother Antonio, his daughter Hero, the waiting gentlewomen Ursula and Margaret, and his witty niece Beatrice. News arrives that Don Pedro of Aragon and his companions are on their way to Messina after a campaign in which they have been victorious. His party includes Claudio and Benedick; the former has shown a decided interest in Hero (which she returns), the latter has long been conducting 'a kind of merry war' with Beatrice. Don Pedro and his party arrive. Claudio sees Hero again, and Beatrice and Benedick are soon skirmishing. The only discordant note is struck by the villainous Don John, the bastard brother of Pedro; despite having been forgiven for siding against Pedro in the recent campaign, he still nurses his grudge.

Much to the cynical Benedick's disgust, Claudio tells Pedro of his love for Hero and asks for his help. Pedro has a plan to help the hesitant and inexperienced lover: at the masked ball that evening he will approach Hero on Claudio's behalf and smooth the way for him. This is overheard by Borachio, one of Don John's henchmen, who persuades his master to wreck Claudio's happiness by making him think Pedro is wooing for himself. The two plans take their course. Although Claudio is quick to believe he has been betrayed, he is as easily disabused by Pedro's assurances that Hero has been 'won' on his behalf. Leonato grants his permission, and a wedding day is agreed upon. Meanwhile, Beatrice has taken the opportunity of disguise to taunt Benedick. Pedro suggests that the friends should amuse themselves by bringing Beatrice and Benedick together.

In the garden the next day Benedick overhears Leonato, Pedro, and Claudio as they talk about Beatrice's hopeless love for him. A similar trick is played on Beatrice, and both of them, convinced that they are the object of a secret passion, resolve to return it.

Meanwhile Don John and Borachio have hatched a far less

genial plot. Margaret, not realising the harm the trick may cause, will disguise herself as her mistress and appear at Hero's window with Borachio. Don John contrives that Claudio and Pedro will see them and draw the obvious conclusion – that Hero is disloyal. Luckily the town Watch, led by the constable Dogberry and his deputy Verges, overhear Borachio boasting to Conrade about all this, but it is not until they have taken the villains to the sexton to be examined that the story comes out, and by then the plot has taken its course. At the wedding Claudio denounces Hero, and is seconded by Pedro and Don John. The distraught Leonato rails at his daughter, but the friar who was to marry the couple, sure that the story must be untrue, suggests that Hero should be hidden until the mystery can be solved, and that in the meantime it should be announced that she is dead. In the emotionally charged aftermath of these events, Beatrice and Benedick suddenly admit their feelings for one another, although the price of love is high for Benedick: he must challenge his friend Claudio to a duel.

Benedick duly confronts Claudio and Pedro, who have already had to deal with the wrath of Leonato and his brother. Then the Watch arrive with their prisoners, and the sexton brings news of Don John's guilt and his flight from Messina. The distraught Claudio is told that he can make some amends by doing penance at Hero's tomb, and by agreeing to marry Antonio's daughter.

Everything is ready for Claudio's wedding to a woman he has never seen – but when she lifts her veil, he discovers that he is to marry Hero after all. After a last moment of hesitation, Benedick and Beatrice are confronted with the sonnets they have secretly written to one another, and they too are to be married. Don John has been captured and brought back to Messina, but there will be time enough to deal with him after the celebrations. 'Strike up, pipers!'

The screenplay

BLACK. A series of lines from a song appear one by one on the screen, in bold white against the darkness. As each LEGEND materialises, we hear a woman's voice speak the line simultaneously.

> VOICE [OFFSCREEN]
> *Sigh no more, ladies* [DISSOLVE],
> *Sigh no more* [DISSOLVE],

The voice is wise, compassionate, knowing. The reading seems personal, read to herself. As if we were merely overhearing it.

> VOICE [OFFSCREEN]
> *Men were deceivers ever* [DISSOLVE],

The rhythm of the dissolves and of the voice is peaceful, steady.

> VOICE [OFFSCREEN]
> *One foot in sea and one on shore* [DISSOLVE],
> *To one thing constant never* [DISSOLVE],

As the next lines follow, we sense a subtle uplift in the voice, an expectancy and lightness that is in sympathy with the unstuffy typeface before us.

> VOICE [OFFSCREEN]
> *Then sigh not so* [DISSOLVE],
> *But let them go* [DISSOLVE],
> *And be you blithe and bonny* [DISSOLVE],
> *Converting all your sounds of woe* [DISSOLVE],
> *Into Hey nonny, nonny!*
> [DISSOLVE TO]

Exterior / **PICNIC SITE** / Day

A misty watercolour painting which fills the entire frame. It is a view of LEONATO'S VILLA. Nestling on top of the hillside, it sits alone, away from Messina itself. Looking more like a rather grand, expansive farmhouse, it suns itself in the beauty of the autumnal late afternoon. The painting shows us the villa's rather crumbling grandeur: the orchard behind, the formal garden to the side, the little chapel, and here and there the farm workers occupied in tending to this self-contained rural Italian paradise. We have dwelt on the painting but a moment until the group laughter has subsided. As it does the VOICE OFFSCREEN begins again. The sounds of the country and a light, as yet distant, musical Air fills the soundtrack as we PAN left to reveal.

Exterior / **PICNIC SITE** / Day

LEONATO'S VILLA itself. We are on a grassy knoll looking up at the actual house.

An idyllic picnic is in progress. As our PAN from the painting across the group proceeds, the VOICE continues, and it becomes clear that the group is being read to.

> VOICE [OFFSCREEN]
> *Sing no more ditties,*
> *Sing no more,*

Into frame comes LEONATO, waistcoat, sun hat, and pleasantly distracted air.

> VOICE [OFFSCREEN]
> *Of dumps so dull and heavy,*

More laughter. We continue our PAN to find HERO.

> VOICE [OFFSCREEN]
> *The fraud of men was ever so,*
> *Since summer first was leafy.*

As the PAN continues, we also PULL out to reveal more of the whole scene, which includes everyone we've seen to date plus FRIAR FRANCIS sitting on a raised path behind the group, gently strumming his guitar, and ANTONIO, LEONATO's brother. Toiling in the background are the VILLA/VINEYARD workers. FOUR YOUNG GIRLS (two household servants, the other two peasants) plus TWO OLDER PEASANT WOMEN are variously distributed among poppies, olive trees, and vines. This group of workers is completed by three men who do most of the labour on LEONATO's estate and who we discover later on will make up THE WATCH, Messina's amateur police force. These men are GEORGE SEACOLE, FRANCES SEACOLE, and HUGH OATCAKE.

> VOICE [OFFSCREEN]
> *Then sigh not so, but let them go,*
> *And be you blithe and bonny,*

We have now PULLED BACK even farther, revealing a tethered donkey and a picnic cloth with the remains of a simple but delicious meal. URSULA, older, elegant, still vivacious, sits at the right of our frame peeling and eating a pear. With the VILLA still in the background, the whole scene looks like an Impressionist painting.

Everyone is now gently chanting the words, but our original voice is drawing closer to us. As our camera finishes its reveal of the sun-drenched rural idyll, strong in LEFT FOREGROUND, book in hand, from which she reads the last lines, emerges the glorious red-haired profile of BEATRICE.

BEATRICE
Converting all your sounds of woe,
Into Hey nonny, nonny!

She finishes with a flourish and the most heartwarming laugh, which turns rather bashful as the others raucously applaud her. Teasing and laughter continue as we CUT.

Exterior / **PICNIC SITE** / Day
LEONATO, laughing away to himself, dabbing at his watercolour. Down the hillside path towards camera is galloping a young male rider. He covers the ground like the wind and pulls up sharply beside LEONATO, who, aware of his approach, has begun to clean brushes and tidy up.

Exterior / **PICNIC SITE** / Day
On THE MESSENGER as he dismounts and hands a letter to LEONATO.

MESSENGER
My lord.

He reads for a moment. His jaw drops. He takes a moment, then slowly to the group of women,

LEONATO
I learn in this letter that Don Pedro of
Arragon comes this night to Messina.

There is the briefest of pauses before everyone (LEONATO included) lets out an enormous scream. Petite pandemonium.

MESSENGER
He is very near by this. He was not three
leagues off when I left him.
LEONATO
How many gentlemen have you lost in this action?
MESSENGER
But few of any sort, and none of name.

LEONATO nods solemnly.

LEONATO [Referring back to the note]
I find here that Don Pedro hath bestowed
much honour on a young Florentine
called Claudio.

There is much wicked 'oooing' at this from HERO, MARGARET, and URSULA. As they exchange laughs, looks, and leers, THE MESSENGER tries to maintain his youthful composure.

MESSENGER
He hath borne himself beyond the promise of his age,
doing in the figure of a lamb, the feats of a lion.

Something of a lamb himself, he stands a little apart and a little uneasy, having now delivered his news. The others continue to clear away, but he finds himself fixed by the defiantly provocative stare of BEATRICE, who has refrained from all of this hub-bubbing and sits exactly where she was when he arrived. She begins with ominous politeness.

BEATRICE
Is Signior Mountanto returned
from the wars or no?

The other girls' ears prick up. THE MESSENGER shifts uneasily.

MESSENGER
I know none of that name, lady.

Stifled giggles begin to be heard as HERO in mid-tidy almost laughs the following into THE MESSENGER's ear as she rushes past him.

HERO
My cousin means Signior Benedick of Padua.

THE MESSENGER first startled, then relieved.

MESSENGER
O, he's returned; and as pleasant as ever he was.
BEATRICE
I pray you, how many hath he killed and eaten
in these wars? But how many hath he killed?
For indeed I promised to eat all of his killing.

THE MESSENGER grows bold and rather proud.

MESSENGER
He hath done good service. And a good
soldier too, lady.

THE MESSENGER is delicious honey to BEATRICE's smiling Bee.

BEATRICE
And a good soldier to a lady. But what is he
to a lord?
MESSENGER [*Uncomfortable*]
A lord to a lord, a man to a man;
stuffed with all honourable virtues.

BEATRICE
It is so, indeed: he is no less than a stuffed man.

General hilarity, during which LEONATO takes the battered youth aside.
The women's excitement is rising.

LEONATO
You must not, sir, mistake my niece. There is a
kind of merry war betwixt Signior Benedick
and her: they never meet but there's a skirmish
of wit between them.

There is a distant rumble that we begin to be aware of, but there is
no stopping BEATRICE, who is now well into her stride.

BEATRICE
Who is his companion now? He hath every
month a new sworn brother.
MESSENGER
He is most in the company of the right noble
Claudio.
BEATRICE
O Lord, he will hang upon him like a disease.
He is sooner caught than the pestilence, and
the taker runs presently mad. God help the
noble Claudio! If he have caught the Benedick,
it will cost him a thousand pound ere a' be cured.

Renewed laughter, during which the mildly confused young
MESSENGER offers a sheepish grin to BEATRICE.

MESSENGER
I will keep friends with you, lady.

BEATRICE rushes to him and plants a smiling, generous kiss on
his cheek.

BEATRICE
Do, good friend.

With all things gathered it's time to make their return to the Villa.
As BEATRICE lifts her bundle, LEONATO shares an intimate moment
with her.

LEONATO [*Knowingly*]
You will never run mad, niece.
BEATRICE [*Eyes atwinkle*]
No, not till a hot January.

A great cloud of dust heralds the imminent arrival of Horsemen. As one, LEONATO, HERO, MARGARET, URSULA, BEATRICE, THE MESSENGER, THE DONKEY, and the OTHER SERVANTS start to make down the hillside to reach the Villa in time to welcome their guests. As we watch their manic retreat, we hear, screamed,

> **MESSENGER**
> *Don Pedro is approaching!*

The CREDITS begin to roll over the following sequence of rapid intercutting between the men and the women. Drums will lead us into the full orchestral accompaniment. The mood is glorious, celebratory, fun!

Exterior / **DIRT ROAD** / Day

Road and sky and heat haze. All we can hear is the drumming of hooves. The flutter of two flags appears, over the crest of the road. CUT.

Exterior / **HILLSIDE** / Day

Wide shot looking up at the top of the hill. A moment of silence before, Geronimo-like, all the women and other picnickers surge over the top towards us. We CUT in to see each individual CLOSE, as they bound down the hill. A mixture of REAL TIME and SLOW MOTION.

Exterior / **DIRT ROAD** / Day

Close on horses' hooves and rippling horseflesh. A mixture of REAL TIME and SLOW MOTION. CUT.

Exterior / **DIRT ROAD** / Day

At last, over the brow of the road, fully revealed, are DON PEDRO and his men. Riding through a mist of dust and heat haze, they look like a combination of Omar Sharif riding into *Lawrence of Arabia* and *The Magnificent Seven*. They ride abreast spanning the width of the road and our screen. With tight leather trousers and boots, a mixture of sweaty shirts and military jackets, they canter in uniform rhythm as one beast.

Exterior / **CYPRESS ALLEY** / Day

Through a gap in this alley of tall trees we see HUGH OATCAKE and the other picnickers race up the hillside. As they reach the gap, we PAN right and let the STEADICAM follow BEATRICE, HERO, and Company as they run down the dip in the alley and up the other side towards the house. The STEADICAM chases them. Runs in front of them. Gives us their point of view.

Exterior / **VINEYARD** / Day

The horsemen in the distance. We RACK FOCUS to see FRANCES SEACOLE running breathlessly towards us. As he flies past camera, we PAN and TRACK left at great speed along parallel lines of vines stretching down the hill away from us. Up each of the alleys come roaring our increasingly fatigued picnickers. A panting and wheezing LEONATO brings up the rear.

Exterior / **DIRT ROAD** / Day

WIDE SHOT of DON PEDRO'S men.

Exterior / **DON PEDRO'S POINT OF VIEW OF VILLA FROM THE ROAD** / Day

We see frantic activity in front of the Villa. Farm workers scurry around, and on the highest roof we see a flag of welcome raised. CUT. CLOSE on GEORGE SEACOLE raising flag. CLOSE on the flag.

Exterior / **DIRT ROAD** / Day

Wide shot reaction to the flag being raised. All six lead riders throw their arms in the air, as one. CUT to

Interior / **WOMEN'S BEDROOM** / Day

STEADICAM moving frantically in this large, uncluttered, cool, dormitory-style bedroom. Catching clothes as they fly through the air. Watching bodices being undone, female flesh being released all over.

Exterior / **DIRT ROAD** / Day

A collection of shots close on the riders. Some real time, some slow motion. Chests heaving. Taut leather thighs against horseflesh. Deeply tanned biceps and pectorals.

Exterior / **ROAD** / Day

Introductory CLOSE-UPS on all the riders. DON PEDRO is in the centre riding in front, a natural commander. All muscle. To his right, CLAUDIO, very young, very beautiful, nervous. To DON PEDRO's left, his brother DON JOHN, THE BASTARD, sexy, dark, reserved. By his side, CONRADE, part of their entourage, young and ferociously fit. To the right of CLAUDIO, BORACHIO, the cocky sidekick to DON JOHN. On the far right of the group, blond, smiling, and warmest of all is BENEDICK, who is clearly leading the fun and excitement.

Interior / **WOMEN'S SHOWER ROOM** / Day

The STEADICAM races down the centre of this primitive shower cubicle. On either side huge leather bags of water are dousing the women, who occasionally streak across in front of camera to steal soap or splash the others. The camera meanwhile continues its progress to the end of the room and the enormous window with a view out to the front of the Villa. The horsemen are rounding a corner of the road, almost at the Villa itself.

Interior / **WOMEN'S SHOWER ROOM**
CLOSE on breasts and backs being lathered.

Exterior / **WASH HOUSE** / Day
Whoosh! From behind we see one of the riders leap straight off his horse and into the elaborate Wash House, which serves as the laundry and refreshment centre for the Villa. A series of quick cuts follow, in which we see – leather trousers and boots being hauled off. A mixture of REAL TIME and SLOW MOTION – chests and buttocks being lathered. The men splashing each other with wild abandon, all in the tank bar DON PEDRO and DON JOHN. The former is redressed by an attendant. The latter stands apart, apparently unmoved by the scene.

Interior / **WOMEN'S BEDROOM** / Day
CLOSE on a pleasing cleavage, which is then dabbed with a huge powder puff and then, by the pull of some strings, is yanked together into an even more fulsome display. We tilt up quickly to see the delighted face of MARGARET observing herself in the mirror. HERO is fixing her hair while URSULA ties her dress at the back. The room is abustle with the other picnicking female servants rushing hither and thither. BEATRICE attempts to maintain a relative indifference to this but continues to make up her toilet and is not averse to the odd shriek.

Interior / **LEONATO'S ROOM** / Day
LEONATO struggling to get into an old pair of 'good' trousers, which have mysteriously shrunk over the years. The attempt causes him to fall over. He gets up to shout at and hit his servant. ANTONIO is laughing at this and fixing his own jacket at the same time. He sniffs under his armpit.

Exterior / **WASH HOUSE** / Day
We TRACK along the front of the arched facade with the men pulling shirts on and doing up trousers (leather and equally tight), attended by some menservants who brought up the rear in supply carts. Be-bronzed, be-silken, damp hair glinting in the sun with

still enough firm flesh on show to have an effect, the men start
to assemble.

Exterior / **INNER COURTYARD VILLA** / Day

Leonato and the women rushing across the upper loggia that looks
into the Courtyard. They hear a trumpet from outside.

Exterior / **WASH HOUSE** / Day

Close on Don Pedro as he motions the others to form up behind him
in the pedestrian version of the symmetrical arrowhead of before. We
watch them climb the steps from the Wash House up to the
formal Garden.

Exterior / **INNER COURTYARD VILLA** / Day

Leonato and all the picnickers gather in a formal group as they wait
for the men.

Exterior / **FORMAL GARDEN** / Day

The Steadicam races towards the formal grouping of soldiers as they
march towards camera. They make a sharp, disciplined left turn and
continue to the great double doors. We follow and halt sharply as
they do.

Exterior / **INNER COURTYARD VILLA** / Day

The huge doors fill our frame. Across them appears the last credit of
the title sequence. The whole opening section has proceeded to this
point like a funny and brisk musical mating dance. End of
opening Credits.

Exterior / **INNER COURTYARD VILLA** / Day

Formal Top Shot of the two groups approaching each other.

Exterior / **INNER COURTYARD VILLA** / Day

The doors open. Don Pedro steps forward. So does Leonato.
These two are old friends.

> **Don Pedro**
> *Good Signior Leonato, are you come to meet*
> *your trouble? The fashion of the world is to*
> *avoid cost, and you encounter it.*
> **Leonato** [*warmly*]
> *Never came trouble to my house*
> *in the likeness of your grace.*

An audible 'Ah' from the household group followed by gentle applause as the two men hug. This is a cue for the groups to loosen up. Hot looks begin to be exchanged between the men and women.

Exterior / **INNER COURTYARD VILLA** / Day / DON PEDRO'S Group

> **DON PEDRO** [to Leonato, indicating HERO]
> *I think this is your daughter.*
> **LEONATO**
> *Her mother hath many times told me so.*

Laughter all around. BENEDICK sees his opportunity.

> **BENEDICK**
> *Were you in doubt, sir, that you asked her?*

Even more amusement. LEONATO laughs the next line as he leads DON PEDRO away for more introductions.

> **LEONATO**
> *Signior Benedick, no!*

The groups are beginning to disperse, and BENEDICK begins to make his way towards the clearly HERO-struck CLAUDIO. His jabber begins almost to himself.

> **BENEDICK**
> *If Signior Leonato be her father, she would not*
> *have his head on her shoulders for all Messina,*
> *as like him as she is.*

He has failed to distract CLAUDIO's attention, but someone has heard him and forces him into the following semi-public skirmish, conducted against the to-ing and fro-ing of the household and visitor traffic.

> **BEATRICE**
> *I wonder that you will still be talking,*
> *Signior Benedick. Nobody marks you.*

Stopping first to 'act' trying to discover where the sound has come from, he turns to face her.

> **BENEDICK** [Innocent]
> *What, my dear Lady Disdain!*
> *Are you yet living?*
> **BEATRICE**
> *Is it possible disdain should die while she*
> *hath such meet food to feed it as Signior*
> *Benedick? Courtesy itself must convert to*
> *disdain if you come in her presence.*

BENEDICK

Then is courtesy a turncoat. But it is certain
I am loved of all ladies, only you excepted; and
I would I could find in my heart that I had not
a hard heart; for truly, I love none.

BEATRICE

A dear happiness to women: they would else
have been troubled with a pernicious suitor. I
thank God and my cold blood, I am of your
humour for that. I had rather hear my dog bark
at a crow than a man swear he loves me.

BENEDICK

God keep your ladyship still in that mind, so
some gentlemen or other shall 'scape a
pre-destinate scratched face.

Now the gloves are really off. The crowd begins to prick up.

BEATRICE

Scratching could not make it worse, an 'twere
such a face as yours.

BENEDICK [*Outraged*]

Well, you are a rare parrot teacher.

BEATRICE [*No mercy*]

A bird of my tongue is better than
a beast of yours.

She's laid herself open.

BENEDICK

I would my horse had the speed of your tongue!

She tries to retaliate. Too late. The crowd has laughed. He swishes
away out of arm's and tongue's length to rejoin DON PEDRO.

BENEDICK

But keep you way, i'God's name. I have done.

CLOSE on BEATRICE. Her face sad, knowing. She speaks almost
to herself.

BEATRICE

You always end with a jade's trick. I know
you of old.

Exterior / **INNER COURTYARD VILLA** / Day / The Whole Group

DON PEDRO in public voice addresses all his men. Everyone
stands attentive. This is important news.

DON PEDRO
Signior Claudio and Signior Benedick, my dear
friend Leonato hath invited you all.

Much 'oooing' and gasping. The girls and boys are in for some
fun, but for how long?

DON PEDRO
I tell him we shall stay here at the least a month.

Applause and delight all round. We feature CLOSE-UPS on CLAUDIO'S,
HERO'S, BEATRICE'S, and BENEDICK'S reactions. LEONATO comes forward
to DON JOHN, who alone has been standing a little to one side, his
frosty presence having kept everyone at bay. This introduction also
becomes a piece of theatre for the group.

LEONATO
Let me bid you welcome, my lord: being
reconciled to the prince your brother, I owe
you all duty.

A breathless pause filled with worried looks. A beat, then DON JOHN
goes to LEONATO.

DON JOHN
I thank you. [The crowd continues to hold its breath]
I am not of many words, but I thank you.

An almost audible sigh of relief passes through the group. LEONATO
leads a gentle progress back into the main house.

LEONATO [*To* DON PEDRO]
Please it your grace lead on?
DON PEDRO
Your hand, Leonato; we will go together.

BENEDICK and CLAUDIO are left beside one of the courtyard wells.
BENEDICK immediately sits on it and pours himself a drink. CLAUDIO is
deeply smitten and stands rooted to the spot gazing after the
retreating HERO, who throws him back a glance.

Exterior / **INNER COURTYARD MAIN WELL** / Day

CLAUDIO
Benedick, didst thou note the daughter of
Signior Leonato?
BENEDICK
I noted her not, but I looked on her.

CLAUDIO
Is she not a modest young lady?
BENEDICK
*Do you question me, as an honest man should
do, for my simple true judgment? Or would you
have me speak after my custom, as being a
professed tyrant to their sex?*
CLAUDIO
No; I pray thee speak in sober judgment.
BENEDICK
*Why, i'faith, methinks she's too low for a
high praise, too brown for a fair praise, and
too little for a great praise. Only this
commendation I can afford her, that were she
other than she is, she were unhandsome; and
being no other than as she is* (He pauses for effect after
this analysis), *I do not like her.*

CLAUDIO will not be beaten down by Benedictine wit, and now that the object of his affection has completely disappeared into the house, he engages with him face to face.

CLAUDIO
*Thou thinkest I am in sport. I pray thee
tell me truly how thou likest her.*

BENEDICK turns to look at him with a deliberate, scrutinising gaze.

BENEDICK
Would you buy her that you inquire after her?
CLAUDIO
Can the world buy such a jewel?

This is getting serious.

BENEDICK
*Yea, and a case to put it into. But speak you
this with a sad brow?*

CLAUDIO rises to stare again at the palace that is LEONATO's house.

CLAUDIO
*In mine eye she is the sweetest lady that
ever I looked on.*

BENEDICK also gets up and looks in the same direction, more worried now.

BENEDICK
I can see yet without spectacles and I see
no such matter.

At that moment BEATRICE walks across the upper loggia, and BENEDICK finds himself saying the following almost to himself.

BENEDICK
There's her cousin, an she were not possessed
with a fury, exceeds her as much in beauty as
the first of May doth the last of December.

He shakes himself out of this reverie to turn on his companion.

BENEDICK
But I hope you have no intent to turn husband,
have you?
CLAUDIO [*Solemnly*]
I would scarce trust myself, though I had sworn the
contrary, if Hero would be my wife.

The final straw. BENEDICK'S comic outrage lets rip.

BENEDICK [*Hitting him*]
Is't come to this? Shall I never see a bachelor of
threescore again?

DON PEDRO has returned from the house, glass in hand.

Exterior / **INNER COURTYARD MAIN WELL** / Day

DON PEDRO
Gentlemen, what secret hath held you here, that
you followed not to Leonato's?
BENEDICK
He [pauses, gathers himself] *is 'in love'*
[still contemptuous]. *With who? That is your*
grace's part. With Hero, Leonato's short
daughter.

Before CLAUDIO has a chance to protest, the smiling Don smooths all.

DON PEDRO
Amen if you love her; for the lady is very
well worthy.

The bashful and battered CLAUDIO is still uncertain if he is being taken seriously. BENEDICK is hovering, ready to pounce with bachelor indignation.

CLAUDIO
You speak this to fetch me in, my lord.
DON PEDRO [Kindly]
By my troth, I speak my thought.
CLAUDIO
And in faith, my lord, I spoke mine.
BENEDICK [Desperately]
And, by my two faiths and
troths, my lord, I spoke mine.
CLAUDIO
That I love her, I feel.
DON PEDRO
That she is worthy, I know.

BENEDICK, the mad fly, continues to buzz around them.

BENEDICK
That I neither feel how she should be loved
nor know how she should be worthy, is the
opinion that fire cannot melt out of me. I
will die in it at the stake.
DON PEDRO
Thou wast ever an obstinate heretic in the
despite of beauty.

BENEDICK now warming to his theme, sure of himself. This man has obviously been hurt.

BENEDICK
That a woman conceived me, I thank her; that
she brought me up, I likewise give her most
humble thanks. But that I will hang my bugle
in an invisible baldrick, all women shall
pardon me. I will live a bachelor.
DON PEDRO [Certain]
I shall see thee, ere I die,
look pale with love.

Red rag to a bull.

BENEDICK
With anger, with sickness, or with hunger,
my lord, not with love.
DON PEDRO [Cat-like, teasing]
Well as time shall try:
'In time the savage bull doth bear the yoke.'

BENEDICK
The savage bull may; but if ever the sensible
Benedick bear it, pluck off the bull's horns
and set them in my forehead. And let me be
vilely painted and in such great letters as
they write 'Here is good horse to hire,' let
them signify under my sign 'Here you may see
Benedick the married man.'

The Don changes tack.

DON PEDRO
Benedick, repair to Leonato's: tell him I
will not fail him at supper; for indeed he hath
made great preparation.

BENEDICK nods, in military fashion, to DON PEDRO, stares frostily at CLAUDIO.

BENEDICK [to CLAUDIO]
Examine your conscience.
[Bows] *And so I leave you.*

DON PEDRO and CLAUDIO stroll outside the Villa doors onto the Patio.

Exterior / **VILLA TERRACE** / Sunset
CLAUDIO walks just behind him and begins by adopting an apparently carefree, roundabout manner.

CLAUDIO
Hath Leonato any son, my lord?
DON PEDRO
No child but Hero; she's his only heir.

He turns to face CLAUDIO and speaks with delicacy, simplicity.

DON PEDRO
Dost thou affect her, Claudio?

The flood gates are open.

CLAUDIO
O, my lord,
When you went onward on this ended action,
I looked upon her with a soldier's eye,
That liked, but had a rougher task in hand,
Than to drive liking to the name of love.
But now I am returned and that war thoughts
Have left their places vacant, in their rooms

> *Come thronging soft and delicate desires,*
> *All prompting me how fair young Hero is,*
> *Saying I liked her ere I went to wars.*
> **DON PEDRO** [Amused]
> *Thou wilt be like a lover presently*
> *And tire the hearer with a book of words.*
> [Suddenly very serious]
> *If thou dost love fair Hero, cherish it,*
> *And I will break with her and with her father*
> *And thou shalt have her.* [Pause, smiles again]

The speechless CLAUDIO breaks into a broad grin. DON PEDRO
continues, miles ahead of him.

> **DON PEDRO**
> *I know we shall have revelling tonight.*
> *I will assume thy part in some disguise*
> *And tell fair Hero I am Claudio,*
> *And in her bosom I'll unclasp my heart*
> *And take her hearing prisoner with the force*
> *And strong encounter of my amorous tale;*
> *Then after to her father will I break;*
> *And the conclusion is, she shall be thine!*
> *In practise let us put it presently.*

After a short beat a previously hidden BORACHIO comes strongly into
frame. He has obviously overheard everything. As he beams a smile,
we DISSOLVE from the smile to

Interior / **DON JOHN'S ROOM** / Night

Low light, candles. We TRACK towards DON JOHN stretched out on a
slab, naked, face down. CONRADE massages him as gently as
possible. This is not a man to cross. CONRADE ventures a remark.

> **CONRADE**
> *What the good year, my lord! Why are you*
> *thus out of measure sad?*

We are close on the dead eyes of the saturnine lord as his head lolls
on the slab.

> **DON JOHN**
> *There is no measure in the occasion that breeds;*
> *therefore the sadness is without limit.*
> **CONRADE** [Pleading]
> *You should hear reason.*

DON JOHN [Annoyed]
And when I have heard it, what
blessing brings it? [Sits up]
I cannot hide what I am. I must be sad when
I have cause and smile at no man's jests; eat
when I have stomach and wait for no man's
leisure; sleep when I am drowsy and tend on no
man's business; laugh when I am merry and claw
no man in his humour.

The increasingly desperate CONRADE follows him trying to help but only adding to his master's irritation.

CONRADE
Yea, but you must not make the full show of this
till you may do it without controlment. You
have of late stood out against your brother, and
he hath ta'en you newly into his grace, where it
is impossible you should take true root but by
the fair weather that you make yourself.
DON JOHN
I had rather be a canker in a hedge than a rose
in his grace. In this, though I cannot be
said to be a flattering honest man, it must not
be denied but I am a plain-dealing villain.
If I had my mouth, I would bite; if I had my
liberty, I would do my liking. In the meantime
let me be that I am and seek not to alter me.

BORACHIO enters the darkened chambers. He has come from the supper. A mask is over his face. He is drunk.

DON JOHN [Eager]
Borachio, what news?

BORACHIO revels in his role as the teller of tales.

BORACHIO
I can give you intelligence of an intended marriage.
DON JOHN [Eyes ablaze]
Will it serve for any model to build mischief on?
BORACHIO
Marry, it is your brother's right hand.
DON JOHN
The most exquisite Claudio?
BORACHIO
Even he.

DON JOHN
How came you to this?

BORACHIO moves closer for the really juicy gossip. He whispers.

BORACHIO
I heard it agreed upon [dramatically] *that the
prince should woo Hero for himself, and
having obtained her* [beat], *give her to Count Claudio.*
DON JOHN [Pause. Smiles]
*Come, come, let us thither.
This may prove food to my displeasure. That
young start - up hath all the glory of my
overthrow. If I can cross him any way, I bless
myself every way.
You are both sure, and will assist me?*
CONRADE
To the death, my lord.
DON JOHN
Shall we go prove what's to be done?
BORACHIO
We'll wait upon your lordship.

The three malcontents laugh and head towards the feast.

Exterior / **VILLA** / Evening
A luscious Italian sunset.

Interior / **HALL** / Night
LEONATO, HERO, ANTONIO, BEATRICE, MARGARET, and URSULA are walking
towards camera, away from the supper room in the background.
They pause as DON JOHN and Company sweep past them, only
stopping to kiss HERO'S hand, and then on into the dining hall where
the men are preparing for the masque dance. LEONATO glances over
his shoulder at their retreating forms.

LEONATO [Puzzled]
Was not Count John here at supper?
ANTONIO
I saw him not.
BEATRICE [Brows furrowed]
*How tartly that gentleman looks! I never can see him
but I am heart - burned an hour after.*
HERO
He is of a very melancholy disposition.

They walk towards our STEADICAM as the SEACOLES and OATCAKE pass in front to present THE FRIAR with his guitar. These are tonight's entertainers! The place has been strung with fairy lights, stretched between the trees. There are flambeaus, food, wine. The girls adjust the lights and start to select from a group of masks that are on stands. The other party-goers picnic and promenade gently on the lush grass. The conversation about ideal men continues.

> BEATRICE [*Brightening*]
> *He were an excellent man that were made just in the*
> *midway between him and Benedick. The one is too like*
> *an image and says nothing, and the other too like my*
> *lady's eldest son, evermore tattling.*

With this they sweep past camera and out into the Courtyard.

Exterior / **CHAPEL YARD** / Night
They walk into the Chapel Yard.

> LEONATO
> *Then half Signior Benedick's tongue in Count*
> *John's mouth, and half Count John's melancholy*
> *in Signior Benedick's face —*
> BEATRICE [*Laughing*]
> *With a good leg and a good foot, uncle, and money*
> *enough in his purse, such a man would win any woman*
> *in the world — if a' could get her good will.*
> LEONATO [*Sighing*]
> *By my troth, niece, thou wilt never get thee a husband,*
> *if thou be so shrewd of thy tongue.*

BEATRICE ignores this as she moves to the masks. She picks one up. She looks at it and muses.

> BEATRICE
> *Lord, I could not endure a husband with a beard*
> *on his face. I had rather lie in the woollen.*
> LEONATO [*Ironic*]
> *You may light on a husband that hath*
> *no beard.*
> BEATRICE
> *What should I do with him? Dress him in my*
> *apparel and make him my waiting-gentlewoman?*

This causes great hilarity among the now masked girls. BEATRICE moves towards the all-suffering LEONATO to gently reinforce her point.

BEATRICE

*He that hath a beard is more than a youth, and
he that hath no beard is less than a man. And
he that is more than a youth is not for me, and
he that is less than a man, I am not for him.*

ANTONIO [Laughing]

In faith, she's too curst.

LEONATO [Utterly exasperated]

Well, then, go you into hell?

BEATRICE [Sweetly]

*No, but to the gate; and there will
the devil meet me. 'Get you to heaven,
Beatrice, get you to heaven; here's no place for
you maids.' So, away to Saint Peter for the
heavens; he shows me where the bachelors sit,
and there live we as merry as the day is long.*

ANTONIO interrupts the female applause to instruct the
masked HERO.

ANTONIO

*Well, niece, I hope you will be ruled by your
father.*

BEATRICE [Interrupting]

*Yes, faith; it is my cousin's duty to make
curtsy and say, 'Father, as it please you.'
But yet for all that, cousin, let him be a
handsome fellow or else make another
curtsy and say, 'Father, as it please me.'*

LEONATO takes HERO to one side to avoid this barrage of filial
insurrection. The drum has started, heralding the imminent arrival of
the masked males for the dance. He speaks hurriedly.

LEONATO

*Daughter, remember what I told you: if the
prince do solicit you in that kind, you know
your answer.*

This done, he turns for one last wistful glance at BEATRICE. Shakes
his head.

LEONATO

*Well, niece. I hope to see you one day fitted
with a husband.*

BEATRICE [Meeting his gaze squarely]

Not till God make men of some other metal than earth.

Touché. LEONATO smiles and gives her the look of a wise old
fellow owl.

> **LEONATO**
> *Cousin, you apprehend passing shrewdly.*
> **BEATRICE** [*Not letting him off the hook*]
> *I have a good eye, uncle; I can see a church*
> *by daylight.*

From the doors to the house there is a great whoosh of male
voices followed by the crash of dancing music. As the girls jump
and scatter, LEONATO yells above the din.

> **LEONATO**
> *The revellers are entering!*

Exterior / **CHAPEL YARD** / Night / The Dance
The effect is a kaleidoscope of coloured lights and faces and
musical instruments. We TRACK violently into the main doors of the
Chapel Yard, where the six men are mysteriously cloaked and
masked. Buttoned up and impossible to tell apart, they swish into
a dramatic entrance position with obvious relish. Breaking out of
this first appearance is DON PEDRO.

> **DON PEDRO** [*to* HERO]
> *Lady, will you walk about with your friend?*

He leads her off under one of the trees.

A MONTAGE OF MYSTERIOUS MASKS AND MUSIC
The party in full swirl.

Exterior / **CHAPEL YARD** / Night
We catch our next couple in the middle of a travelling grope.
URSULA indulges ANTONIO, while slapping his hands away. His
subterfuge is not working. She tugs on his mask.

> **URSULA**
> *I know you well enough; you are Signior Antonio.*
> **ANTONIO** [*He could be no one else*]
> *At a word, I am not.*
> **URSULA**
> *I know you by the waggling of your head.*

He stops waggling his head.

> **ANTONIO**
> *At a word, I am not.*

He is so frustrated, he is practically stamping.

> **URSULA**
> *Come, come, do you think I do not know you by*
> *your excellent wit? Can virtue hide itself?*
> *Go to, mum, you are he: graces will appear, and*
> *there's an end.*

This mollifies him. They run off.

Exterior / **CHAPEL YARD** / Night

The ever ample cleavage of MARGARET dances into view under the gaze of BORACHIO. They are both drunk and giggly.

> **BORACHIO**
> *...Well, I would you did like me.*
> **MARGARET**
> *So would not I, for I have many ill qualities.*
> **BORACHIO**
> *Which is one?*
> **MARGARET**
> *I say my prayers aloud.*

She finds this unspeakably funny and barks herself off into the darkness whilst the gropery of her partner goes on apace.

Exterior / **CHAPEL YARD** / Night / Drinking Fountain

BEATRICE charges into view, all pretence of using her mask having been abandoned as she pursues BENEDICK'S seedy Mr. Punch. A madly grinning face is spewing water out of a wall and into a stone basin in front. Apples and pears are bobbing wildly, but not as wildly as BEATRICE, who stands on one side of the spray facing BENEDICK, who is on the other.

> **BEATRICE**
> *Will you not tell me who told you?*
> **BENEDICK** [*In a heavily disguised accent*]
> *No, you shall pardon me.*

Pause. Frustration. This is not working. Tries again.

> **BEATRICE**
> *Nor will you not tell me who you are?*
>
> **BENEDICK**
> *Not now.*

Musing, through gritted teeth.

BEATRICE
That I was disdainful, and that I had my good
wit out of the 'Hundred Merry Tales' – well,
[surprise, surprise] *this was Signior Benedick*
that said so.

The ears of the mask appear to prick up. He looks, she is still
standing by the grinning water fountain staring, apparently idly, out
at the couples dancing.

BENEDICK
What's he?
BEATRICE [Nonchalant]
I am sure you know him well enough.

He works hard to feign disinterest.

BENEDICK
Not I, believe me.
BEATRICE
Did he never make you laugh?

More gritted teeth.

BENEDICK
I pray you, what is he?
BEATRICE [With relish]
Why, he is the prince's jester. A very dull fool.
His only gift is in devising impossible slanders.
None but libertines delight in him; for he both
pleases men and angers them, and then they
laugh at him and beat him.

BENEDICK is now a slumped man. She begins to take pity.

BEATRICE
I am sure he is in the fleet.

She begins to go, then turns to look him right in the semi-masked
eye with naughty intents.

BEATRICE
I would he had boarded me.

Despite being rather hotly disturbed by her boldness, he will not
have his humiliation bought off with bawdiness. He barks at her.

BENEDICK
When I know the gentleman, I'll tell him what
you say.

She is smiling, radiant and irresistible. She almost kisses the next words at him.

> **BEATRICE**
> *Do, do.*

The music is drawing to an end. She looks at the house where the others are headed for refreshment.

> **BEATRICE**
> *We must follow the leaders.*

He is relieved to escape.

> **BENEDICK**
> *In every good thing.*

Exterior / **CHAPEL YARD** / Night

CLOSE on an anxious CLAUDIO as he watches DON PEDRO promenade with HERO. We see his POINT OF VIEW.

Exterior / **CHAPEL YARD** / Night

The crowd tangos. Among them, a little apart, the understandably anxious CLAUDIO, who has watched from afar the prince's wooing on his behalf. DON JOHN and BORACHIO emerge from the shadows. They move with great urgency to the man they know to be CLAUDIO. DON JOHN speaks in a highly convincing panicked whisper.

> **DON JOHN**
> *Are not you Signior Benedick?*

CLAUDIO decides to play along. This is clearly important, serious.

> **CLAUDIO** [*Assuming* BENEDICK'S *voice*]
> *You know me well, I am he.*
> **DON JOHN**
> *Signior, you are very near my brother in his love:* [dramatically] *he is enamoured on Hero.*

He feels CLAUDIO buckle.

> **DON JOHN**
> *I pray you dissuade him from her: she is no equal for his birth.*
> **CLAUDIO** [Desperate]
> *How know you he loves her?*
> **DON JOHN**
> *I heard him swear his affection.*
> **BORACHIO**
> *So did I too; and he swore he would marry her tonight.*

DON JOHN
Come, let us to the banquet.

Exterior / **CHAPEL YARD** / Night

CLAUDIO speaks to himself in a muffled torrent of words, almost sick.

CLAUDIO
Thus answer I in name of Benedick,
But hear these ill news with the ears of Claudio.
'Tis certain so: the prince woos for himself!
Friendship is constant in all other things
Save in the office and affairs of love.

He spits out the last word. He continues, grimly ironic.

CLAUDIO
This is an accident of hourly proof,
Which I mistrusted not. Farewell, therefore,
Hero!

Exterior / **CHAPEL YARD** / Night

CLAUDIO storms off and bumps into BENEDICK.

BENEDICK
Count Claudio?

CLAUDIO looks away. Replies, barely audibly.

CLAUDIO
Yea, the same.

BENEDICK motions to the house.

BENEDICK
Come, will you go with me?

Still looking away,

CLAUDIO
Whither?

This is getting tedious for BENEDICK. He speaks as if to a deaf man.

BENEDICK
About your own business.

Still waiting for some response. There is none. He decides to tell the news anyway.

BENEDICK
The prince hath got your Hero!

CLAUDIO lashes back bitterly.

CLAUDIO
I wish him joy of her!

This is beginning to make sense to BENEDICK. He sighs and looks askance at his young friend, who is becoming more worked up. He has a very low opinion of CLAUDIO's behaviour. He's seen it all before.

BENEDICK
Did you think the prince would have served you
thus?
CLAUDIO [Exploding with passion]
I pray you, leave me!

BENEDICK breathes an enormous sigh, as CLAUDIO storms off into the night. He looks after him and shakes his head.

Exterior / **CHAPEL YARD** / Night

BENEDICK
Alas, poor hurt fowl.

Then, returning to his own preoccupation,

BENEDICK
But that my Lady Beatrice should know me,
and not know me! [Contemptuously] *The prince's base,*
fool! Ha? I am not so reputed. It is the base
though bitter, disposition of Beatrice that puts
the world into her person, and so gives me out.
Well, I'll be revenged as I may.

He starts off determinedly but is prevented from completing his mission of revenge by the arrival of DON PEDRO and HERO.

Exterior / **CHAPEL YARD** / Night

DON PEDRO
Now, signior, where's the count?
BENEDICK
Troth, my lord, I found him here as melancholy
as a lodge in a warren. I told him, and I think
I told him true, that your grace had got the
good will of this young lady.

He bows, news delivered, and begins to leave. After a swift, mischievous look between HERO and DON PEDRO, the latter raises his voice to call his friend back again.

DON PEDRO [Mock outrage]
The Lady Beatrice hath a quarrel
to you. The gentleman that danced with her told
her she is much wronged by you.

BENEDICK is stopped in his tracks. He turns and rushes back to the
prince, exploding and spluttering all the way. This woman is under
his skin.

BENEDICK
O, she misused me past the endurance of a
block! She told me, not thinking I had been
myself, that I was the prince's jester,

HERO and DON PEDRO struggle to maintain their sympathetic looks,
battling against a sea of giggles. BENEDICK becomes more animated
and hurt.

BENEDICK
that I was duller than a great thaw, huddling
jest upon jest with such impossible conveyance
upon me that I stood like a man at a mark, with
a whole army shooting at me. She speaks
poniards, and every word stabs. If her breath were
as terrible as her terminations, there were no living
near her; she would infect to the north star.

HERO and DON PEDRO have to turn away, but BENEDICK barks them back
to attention with yet more frustration.

BENEDICK
So indeed, all disquiet, horror, and
perturbation follows her.

BENEDICK is now facing DON PEDRO and so cannot see the approach of
a familiar group. DON PEDRO plays the ace.

DON PEDRO
Look, here she comes.

BENEDICK does not even turn round. His eyes close briefly, then after
the smallest beat he begins his urgent, intimate, forlorn plea to
the prince.

BENEDICK
Will your grace command me any service to
the world's end?

Reaction on BEATRICE, who has just managed to catch this. As the comically desperate BENEDICK continues his futile plea to the immovable prince, BEATRICE'S group, including LEONATO, ANTONIO, URSULA, and CLAUDIO, all move closer. BENEDICK'S nose is almost touching DON PEDRO'S as he continues a feeble whisper.

> **BENEDICK**
> *I will go on the slightest errand now to the Antipodes that you can devise to send me on. I will fetch you a hair off the Great Cham's beard,*

Grasping now for any deed that will make an impact.

> **BENEDICK**
> *do you any embassage to the Pigmies, rather than hold three words' conference with this harpy.*

Reaction on BEATRICE. DON PEDRO is unflinching. His eyes give the answer. BENEDICK shakes his head, gives a wry smile, defeated.

> **BENEDICK**
> *You have no employment for me?*

> **DON PEDRO** [Laughing]
> *None, but to desire your good company!*

He pats BENEDICK on the back.

> **BENEDICK**
> *O God, sir, here's a dish I love not. I cannot endure my Lady Tongue!*

Exterior / **CHAPEL YARD** / Night
The atmosphere has changed. DON PEDRO'S laugh has faded in the face of BEATRICE'S troubled look. He attempts to gently tease her out of it.

> **DON PEDRO**
> *Come, lady, come; you have lost the heart of Signior Benedick.*

She returns the smile, but the tone is rueful, rather sad. She's aware of the others listening and is shy.

> **BEATRICE**
> *Indeed, my lord, he lent it me a while, and I gave him use for it, a double heart for his single one. Marry, once before he won it of me, with false dice, therefore your grace may well say I have lost it.*

This gravity is more than he bargained for. He tries again with a gentle goad.

> **DON PEDRO**
> *You have put him down, lady, you have put him down.*

She rises to it this time.

> **BEATRICE**
> *So I would not he should do me, my lord, lest*
> *I should prove the mother of fools.*

This is the merry lady. Fully recovered, she now gets on with the tricky business in hand.

> **BEATRICE**
> *I have brought Count Claudio, whom you sent me*
> *to seek.*

CLAUDIO rather sulkily steps forward. DON PEDRO and HERO are confused.

> **DON PEDRO**
> *Why, how now, count, wherefore are you*
> *sad?*

CLAUDIO will not look at him.

> **CLAUDIO**
> *Not sad, my lord.*
> **DON PEDRO** [Genuinely concerned]
> *How then? Sick?*
> **CLAUDIO**
> *Neither, my lord.*

BEATRICE enters the fray with her customary zeal. HERO has not reacted well to this conversation.

> **BEATRICE**
> *The count is neither sad, nor sick, nor merry,*
> *nor well, but civil count, civil as an orange,*
> *and something of that* jealous *complexion.*

The truth dawns slowly on DON PEDRO.

> **DON PEDRO**
> *I' faith, lady, I think your blazon to be true,*
> *though I'll be sworn, if he be so, his conceit*
> *is false.* [Warmly, kind] *Here, Claudio, I have*
> *wooed in thy name, and fair Hero is won.*

CLOSE-UPS on the vulnerably questioning look of CLAUDIO and the eagerly returned look from the nodding, smiling HERO. CLAUDIO looks again to the prince. Is it true?

DON PEDRO
I have broke with her father and his good will obtained.
Name the day of marriage, and God give thee joy.

CLAUDIO's head is beginning to swim. LEONATO also takes pity and speaks gently but with great dignity.

LEONATO
Count, take of me my daughter, and with her
my fortunes. His grace hath made the match,
and all grace say Amen to it.

The longest silence. Moist-eyed smiles from the onlookers. Tear-stained cheeks on the faces of the two lovers, now rapt in each other. The silence continues.

BEATRICE
Speak, count, 'tis your cue.

His eyes are locked on HERO. He is rooted to the spot, like her. He begins, barely audible.

CLAUDIO
Silence is the perfectest herald of joy. I were
but little happy if I could say how much.

He takes a step towards her. Then, solemnly,

CLAUDIO
Lady, as you are mine, I am yours.
BEATRICE
Speak, cousin! Or, if you cannot, stop his mouth with
a kiss, and let not him speak, either.

The joy is infectious. They kiss and the others laugh, cheer, and clap. HERO and CLAUDIO move a little aside. The others also withdraw a little to give the young couple this moment.

DON PEDRO
In faith, lady, you have a merry
heart.
BEATRICE
Yea, my lord, I thank it. Poor fool, it keeps
on the windy side of care.

Exterior / **CHAPEL YARD** / Night

Don Pedro and Beatrice watch the young lovers whispering to each other, while Leonato quietly instructs some of the servants in the clearing-up operation. The musicians still play and sing and promenade. The mood is joyous but tinged with a strange melancholy.

> **Beatrice**
> *My cousin tells him in his ear that he is in her heart.*

Claudio hears this and responds laughing, excited. He calls to Beatrice.

> **Claudio**
> *And so she doth, cousin.*

The lovers move farther away from potential teasing and leave us to the quiet between Don Pedro and Beatrice. She speaks, almost to herself.

> **Beatrice**
> *Good Lord, for alliance! Thus goes everyone to*
> *the world but I, and I am sunburnt. I may sit in*
> *a corner and cry 'Heigh-ho for a husband.'*
> **Don Pedro**
> *Lady Beatrice, I will get you one.*
> **Beatrice**
> *I would rather have one of your father's*
> *getting. Hath your grace ne'er a brother like*
> *you? Your father got excellent husbands, if a*
> *maid could come by them.*
> **Don Pedro** [Gently]
> *Will you have me, lady?*

The atmosphere has changed completely. The tenderness and vulnerability of the prince's remark remind Beatrice that they have found themselves uncomfortably alone.

> **Beatrice** [Delicately]
> *No, my lord, unless I might have another for working*
> *days. Your grace is too costly to wear every day.*

Don Pedro looks away, shy.

> **Beatrice**
> *But I beseech your grace, pardon me. I was born*
> *to speak all mirth and no matter.*

He comes round again with a smile.

DON PEDRO
Your silence most offends me, and to be merry
best becomes you; for out o' question, you were
born in a merry hour.

BEATRICE is now struck and looks away.

BEATRICE [*Quietly*]
No, sure, my lord, my mother cried.
But then there was a star danced, and under
that was I born.

Before allowing herself to go any further, she gathers herself quickly and runs for the house. Smiling first at DON PEDRO, then yelling to the lovers as she goes.

BEATRICE
Cousins, God give you joy!

Exterior / **CHAPEL YARD** / Night

Close on DON PEDRO. He speaks for himself, semi-regretful but generous.

DON PEDRO
By my troth, a pleasant-spirited lady.

LEONATO catches the last of this as he brings the lovers over to the prince.

LEONATO
There's little of the melancholy element in her,
my lord. She is never sad but when she sleeps,
and not ever sad then; for I have heard my
daughter say she hath often dreamt of
unhappiness and waked herself with laughing.

They all share the joke. DON PEDRO continues to muse.

DON PEDRO
She cannot endure to hear tell of a husband.
LEONATO
O, by no means.

The laughter continues. DON PEDRO cuts across it.

DON PEDRO
She were an excellent wife for Benedick.
LEONATO
O Lord, if they were but a week
married, they would talk themselves mad.

But DON PEDRO is now in action mood. He speaks quickly, to
the point.

> **DON PEDRO**
> *County Claudio, when mean you to go to church?*
> **CLAUDIO** [Passionately]
> *Tomorrow, my lord.*

Yet another shock for the increasingly bewildered and (frankly) quite
tipsy LEONATO.

> **LEONATO**
> *Not till Monday, my dear son, which is hence*
> *a just seven-night, and a time too brief, too,*
> *to have all things answer my mind.*

The crestfallen CLAUDIO is given no time to protest. DON PEDRO is now
in his stride.

> **DON PEDRO**
> *I warrant thee, Claudio, the time shall*
> *not go dully by us. I will in the interim*
> *undertake one of Hercules' labours, which is to*
> *bring Signior Benedick and the Lady Beatrice into*
> *a mountain of affection th' one with th' other.*
> *I would fain have it a match, and I doubt*
> *not but to fashion it, if you three will but*
> *minister such assistance as I shall give you direction.*

LEONATO is now almost hysterical.

> **LEONATO**
> *My lord, I am for you, though it cost me ten*
> *nights' watchings.*
> **CLAUDIO**
> *And I, my lord.*
> **DON PEDRO**
> *And you too, gentle Hero?*
> **HERO**
> *I will do any modest office, my lord, to help*
> *my cousin to a good husband.*

DON PEDRO speaks almost as if taking an oath.

> **DON PEDRO**
> *If we can do this, Cupid is no longer*
> *an archer; his glory shall be ours, for we are*
> *the only love-gods. Go in with me, and I will*
> *tell you my drift.*

Dɪssᴏʟᴠᴇ as they run towards the house, to

Exterior / **LEONATO'S VILLA** / Dawn
Wide establishing shot of the Villa nestling dreamlike in the mist and early light. Dɪssᴏʟᴠᴇ to

Exterior / **FOUNTAIN** / Day
Bᴇɴᴇᴅɪᴄᴋ in Hamlet mode. All preoccupation. During the following speech Bᴇɴᴇᴅɪᴄᴋ attempts to find the right spot for his folding canvas deck chair in relation to the fountain and also attempts to disguise the fact (*through* several attempts) that he doesn't know how to put the chair up.

> **Bᴇɴᴇᴅɪᴄᴋ**
> *I do much wonder that one man, seeing how much*
> *another man is a fool when he dedicates his*
> *behaviours to love, will, after he hath laughed*
> *at such shallow follies in others, become the*
> *argument of his own scorn by falling in love.*

There is a pause. To admit temporary defeat with the deck chair and to consider who that last remark might apply to.

> **Bᴇɴᴇᴅɪᴄᴋ**
> *And such a man is Claudio. I have*
> *known when there was no music with him but the*
> *drum and the fife, and now had he rather hear*
> *the tabor and the pipe. I have known when he*
> *would have walked ten mile afoot to see a good*
> *armour, and now will he lie ten nights awake*
> *carving the fashion of a new doublet. He was*
> *wont to speak plain and to the purpose, like an*
> *honest man and a soldier, and now is he turned*
> *orthography. His words are a very fantastical*
> *banquet, just so many strange dishes.*

As his frustration dies away, so does his interest in the deck chair. He sits on the edge of the fountain and adopts a more ruminative tone.

> **Bᴇɴᴇᴅɪᴄᴋ**
> *May I be so converted, and see with these eyes?*
> *I cannot tell. I think not. I will not be sworn*
> *but love may transform me to an oyster, but I'll*
> *take my oath on it, till he have made an oyster*
> *of me, he shall never make me such a fool.*
> *One woman is fair, yet I am well. Another*

is wise, yet I am well. Another virtuous, yet I
am well. But till all graces be in one woman,
one woman shall not come in my grace. Rich she
shall be, that's certain. Wise, or I'll none.
Virtuous, or I'll never cheapen her. Fair, or
I'll never look on her. Mild, or come not near me.
Of good discourse, an excellent musician – and her
hair shall be of what colour it please God.

He hears the sound of voices. From the other end of a floral alley
DON PEDRO, CLAUDIO, LEONATO, and BALTHASAR and Company
approach. BENEDICK is thrown into panic.

> **BENEDICK**
> *Ha! The prince and Monsieur Love.*

He looks around desperately.

> **BENEDICK**
> *I will hide me.*

He tries behind the hedge.

Exterior / **FLORAL WALK** / Day

On CLAUDIO, DON PEDRO, LEONATO, BALTHASAR, THE FRIAR, THE SEACOLES,
and OATCAKE. We see their point of view of the hapless BENEDICK.
DON PEDRO starts off the game.

> **DON PEDRO**
> *See you where Benedick hath hid*
> *himself?*
> **CLAUDIO** [Whispered]
> *Very well, my lord.*
> **DON PEDRO** [Loud]
> *Come, Balthasar, we'll hear that song again.*

The men sit in the beautiful orange afternoon light as THE FRIAR
plays his guitar. They are grouped about the fountain but
through the slightly damaged hedge can see the skulking form
of BENEDICK.

Exterior / **ORCHARD ALLEY** / Day

Benedick attempts (unsuccessfully) to erect his deck chair in the
narrow alley. He stops as he hears the music begin.

> **BENEDICK** [Ironic]
> *Now, divine air! Now is his soul ravished!*
> *Is it not strange that sheeps' guts*

should hale souls out of men's bodies?

Exterior / **FOUNTAIN** / Day

The camera tracks around the circular fountain as BALTHASAR sings and the lounging nobles breathe an image of deep tranquillity. The camera movement is slow. The music is beautiful, melodic, dancing on the late afternoon air. In the background we can see our household servants. Beyond them the vines, the olive groves, the lush countryside.

> **BALTHASAR**
> *Sigh no more, ladies, sigh no more.*
> *Men were deceivers ever,*
> *One foot in sea, and one on shore,*
> *To one thing constant never.*
> *Then sigh not so, but let them go,*
> *And be you blithe and bonny,*
> *Converting all your sounds of woe*
>
> *Into Hey nonny, nonny.*
> *Sing no more ditties, sing no more,*
> *Of dumps so dull and heavy;*
> *The fraud of men was ever so,*
> *Since summer first was leafy;*
> *Then sigh not so, but let them go,*
> *And be you blithe and bonny,*
> *Converting all your sounds of woe*
> *Into Hey nonny, nonny.*

A pause. DON PEDRO breaks the spell gently.

> **DON PEDRO**
> *By my troth, a good song.*
> **BALTHASAR** [*Modestly*]
> *And an ill singer, my lord.*
> **DON PEDRO** [*Gently*]
> *No, no, faith; thou singest well enough.*

BALTHASAR, THE FRIAR, and the THREE BOYS exit.

Exterior / **ORCHARD ALLEY** / Day

> **BENEDICK**
> *An he had been a dog that*
> *should have howled thus,*
> *they would have hanged him!*

He makes another effort with his deck chair.

Exterior / **FOUNTAIN** / Day

> **DON PEDRO** [*Very loudly*]
> *Come hither, Leonato. What was it you told me of*
> *today, that your niece Beatrice was* in love *with*
> *Signior Benedick?*

Exterior / **ORCHARD ALLEY** / Day

BENEDICK shrieks, falls in, over, and through the deck chair and almost through one of the hedges that form the wall of the alley.

Exterior / **FOUNTAIN** / Day

> **CLAUDIO** [*Loudly*]
> *I did never think that lady would have*
> *loved any man.*
> **LEONATO**
> *No, nor I neither. But most wonderful that she*
> *should so dote on Signior Benedick, whom she*
> *hath in all outward behaviours seemed ever to abhor.*

Exterior / **ORCHARD ALLEY** / Day

Huge CLOSE-UP on an astonished BENEDICK through the hedge.

> **BENEDICK**
> *Is't possible?*

Exterior / **FOUNTAIN** / Day

> **DON PEDRO**
> *Maybe she doth but counterfeit?*
> **CLAUDIO**
> *Faith, like enough.*
> **LEONATO** [*With a great yell*]
> *O God! Counterfeit?*

Exterior / **FOUNTAIN** / Day

DON PEDRO and CLAUDIO stifle their giggles as LEONATO continues, very dramatically, in his stride now.

> **LEONATO**
> *There was never counterfeit of passion came so near*
> *the life of passion as she discovers it.*

They are all smugly delighted with their progress now. DON PEDRO sets LEONATO up for an ever more fulsome display of evidence.

> **DON PEDRO**
> *Why, what effects of passion shows she?*

LEONATO's face begins to pale as a maniacally excited CLAUDIO whispers in his ear.

> **CLAUDIO**
> *Bait the hook well. This fish will bite.*

LEONATO is completely stumped.

Exterior / **FOUNTAIN** / Day

LEONATO now in a cold sweat. Panic setting in on DON PEDRO and CLAUDIO. The star performer is letting them down.

> **LEONATO**
> *What effects, my lord? She will sit you...*
> *you heard my daughter tell you how.*

CLAUDIO clutches at the straw.

> **CLAUDIO**
> *She did indeed.*

DON PEDRO, desperately under pressure, throws the ball back to LEONATO.

> **DON PEDRO**
> *How, how, I pray you?*

LEONATO has a brain wave and whispers into DON PEDRO's ear. He understands LEONATO's plot. He turns away, shakes his head and acts quiet outrage.

> **DON PEDRO**
> *You* amaze *me.*

Exterior / **ORCHARD ALLEY** / Day

BENEDICK looks like a startled deer. What can LEONATO have said?

> **BENEDICK** [Desperately worried]
> *I should think this a trick, but that the white*
> *bearded fellow speaks it.*

Exterior / **FOUNTAIN** / Day

They have all breathed an enormous sigh of relief. BENEDICK is still on the hook. They can now move into a regretful/tragic tone.

> **DON PEDRO**
> *Hath she made her affection known to Benedick?*
> **LEONATO**
> *No, and swears she never will. That's her*
> *torment. She'll be up twenty times a night, and*
> *there will she sit in her smock till she have*

writ a sheet of paper. My daughter tells us she
tore the letter into a thousand halfpence,
railed at herself that she should be so immodest
to write to one that she knew would flout her.

CLAUDIO seizes on this image with relish.

CLAUDIO
Then down upon her knees she falls, weeps, sobs,
 beats her heart, tears her hair, prays, curses,
'O sweet Benedick, God give me patience.'

Exterior / **FOUNTAIN** / Day

LEONATO
She doth indeed, my daughter says so.
My daughter is sometime afeard she will do a
desperate outrage to herself. It is very true.

Pause.

DON PEDRO
It were good that Benedick knew of it.
CLAUDIO
To what end? He would make but a sport of it
and torment the poor lady worse.

They all nod, hem and hah. The mood very sad.

Exterior / **BREAK IN HEDGE** / Day

BENEDICK *not* pleased with this remark.

Exterior / **FOUNTAIN** / Day

LEONATO
I am sorry for her.

Pause.

DON PEDRO
I pray you tell Benedick of it, and hear
what a' will say.
LEONATO [Gravely]
Were it good, think you?
CLAUDIO [With equal gravity]
Hero thinks surely she will die, for she says she will
die if he love her not, and she will die ere she make her
love known, and she will die if he woo her.

DON PEDRO [*Grimly*]
Ay. If she should make tender of her love,
'tis very possible he'll scorn it, for the man,
as you know all, hath a contemptible spirit.

Exterior / **BREAK IN HEDGE** / Day
BENEDICK lets out a grunt of annoyance.

Exterior / **FOUNTAIN** / Day
The trio stop talking to listen.

Exterior / **BREAK IN HEDGE** / Day
BENEDICK, panicked, turns the grunt into a bird noise. Unconvincing.

Exterior / **FOUNTAIN** / Day
The trio do '*Oh, it was only a coyote*' acting.

Exterior / **BREAK IN HEDGE** / Day
BENEDICK sighs with relief.

Exterior / **FOUNTAIN** / Day

DON PEDRO
I love Benedick well, and I could wish he
would modestly examine himself, to see
how much he is unworthy so good a
lady.
LEONATO
My lord, will you walk? Dinner is ready.

The men get up.

Exterior / **FLORAL ALLEY** / Day
The threesome walk towards camera, down the alley away from the
fountain and BENEDICK.

CLAUDIO [*Whispering*]
If he do not dote on her upon
this, I will never trust my expectation.
DON PEDRO
Let there be the same net spread for
her, and that must your daughter and her
gentlewomen carry. Let us send Beatrice to call
him in to dinner.

The three run past camera laughing.

Exterior / **ORCHARD ALLEY** / Day

With some difficulty, BENEDICK's head emerges. A surprised blond thing against the green. He is one astonished soldier.

> **BENEDICK**
> *This can be no trick.*

He looks in the direction of the men.

> **BENEDICK**
> *The conference was sadly borne.*
> *They have the truth of this from Hero.*

He stops for a moment to say the miraculous thing.

> **BENEDICK**
> *Love me?*

Thinks.

> **BENEDICK**
> *Why, it must be requited. I hear how I am*
> *censured. They say I will bear myself proudly if*
> *I perceive the love come from her. They say too*
> *that she will rather die than give any sign of*
> *affection.*

He stops again.

> **BENEDICK**
> *I did never think to marry. I must not seem*
> *proud. Happy are they that hear their*
> *detractions and can put them to mending.*
> *They say the lady is fair. 'Tis a truth, I can*
> *bear them witness. And virtuous, 'tis so, I*
> *cannot reprove it. And wise, but for loving me.*
> *By my troth, it is no addition to her wit, nor*
> *no great argument of her folly, for I will be*
> *horribly in love with her. I may chance have*
> *some odd quirks and remnants of wit broken on me*
> *because I have railed so long against marriage;*
> *but doth not the appetite alter? A man loves the*
> *meat in his youth that he cannot endure in his*
> *age. Shall quips and sentences and these paper*
> *bullets of the brain awe a man from the career*
> *of his humour? No. The world must be peopled.*

All this has been delivered to camera, as he paces the Formal Garden, but he moves forward for this next, frightened that someone might overhear.

> **BENEDICK**
> *When I said I would die a bachelor, I did not*
> *think I should live till I were married.*

A thumping sound from the ground and the sense of a storm
approaching indicate the imminent arrival of an angry person.
BENEDICK runs to the ORCHARD ALLEY to see a marching, nostril-flared,
flame-coloured thing. He turns to camera and shrieks.

> **BENEDICK**
> *Here comes* Beatrice!

Exterior / **FOUNTAIN** / Day

With BEATRICE almost upon him, he calms down and whispers to
camera rather gooily.

> **BENEDICK**
> *By this day, she's a fair lady!*

Then, as an afterthought:

> **BENEDICK**
> *I* do *spy some marks of love in her.*

The sun is now starting to go down, and sits in the sky behind
BEATRICE, who looks glorious in this temper. She stops marching as
she reaches the gap in the ORCHARD ALLEY. She turns sharply to
see BENEDICK.

> **BEATRICE**
> *Against my will I am sent to bid you come in to dinner.*

BENEDICK has thrown what he thinks to be a gallant and sexy leg up
on the edge of the fountain. He strikes a pose and a tone of voice
that reminds one of Tony Curtis as Cary Grant in *Some Like It Hot*.
It is a face frozen in a grin that is trying to convey, sex, romance,
intelligence, wit, and warmth, all at once. In short, he
looks ridiculous.

> **BENEDICK**
> *Fair Beatrice, I thank you for your pains.*

She speaks even more slowly. She is clearly dealing with a
deranged person.

> **BEATRICE**
> *I took no more pains for those thanks than you*
> *take pains to thank me. If it had been painful*
> *I would not have come.*

BENEDICK in love sees the good in everything.

>**BENEDICK**
>*You take pleasure, then, in the message?*
>**BEATRICE**
>*Yea, just so much as you may take upon a*
>*knife's point.*

He laughs hysterically. He *thinks* she's *so* funny. She *knows*
he's certifiable.

>**BEATRICE**
>*You have no stomach, signior? Fare you well.*

She thunders her way back down the ORCHARD ALLEY, and as she
turns out of sight BENEDICK runs up to the gap in the ORCHARD ALLEY,
then turns to camera.

>**BENEDICK**
>*Ha!*

He looks like the cat that got the cream, the milk, the fish, and the
keys to the house.

Exterior / **FOUNTAIN** / Day

>**BENEDICK**
>*'Against my will I am sent to bid you come*
>*in to dinner.'*

Pause.

>**BENEDICK**
>*There's a double meaning in that.*

We CUT.

Exterior / **FORMAL GARDEN** / Day
Another part of the ORCHARD/GARDEN. BEATRICE is still powering back
to the house.

Exterior / **FORMAL GARDEN/ALLEY** / Day
URSULA and HERO wait at the side of the house. As they see BEATRICE
come round the corner at the other end, we TRACK right with them as
they promenade towards another part of the garden.

Exterior / **LADIES' GARDEN** / Day
The duo peeking behind them to spot BEATRICE's progress. When
she's near enough, URSULA rushes back to HERO. URSULA yells,

URSULA
But are you sure
That Benedick loves Beatrice so entirely?

Exterior / **VILLA TERRACE** / Day

Although almost at the house, BEATRICE stops in her tracks. Eyes
on stalks.

Exterior / **LADIES' GARDEN** / Day

BEATRICE's thumping steps have stopped. They know she's listening.

HERO
So says the prince and my new trothed lord.
URSULA
And did they bid you tell her of it, madam?

They begin to walk. BEATRICE rushes to head them off and hides
inside a nest of topiary trees; she is in the middle, perched on a tiny
footbridge, which spans a small ornamental pool.

HERO
They did entreat me to acquaint her of it,
But I persuaded them, if they loved Benedick,
To wish him wrestle with affection
And never to let Beatrice know of it.
URSULA
Why did you so? Doth not the gentleman
Deserve as full as fortunate a bed
As ever Beatrice shall couch upon?
HERO
O god of love! I know he doth deserve
As much as may be yielded to a man.
But nature never framed a woman's heart
Of prouder stuff than that of Beatrice.

BEATRICE is inside this circular feature, the girls are walking around
its perimeter, each trying to avoid the gaze of the other.

HERO
Disdain and scorn ride sparkling in her eyes,
Misprising what they look on, and her wit
Values itself so highly that to her
All matter else seems weak. She cannot love.

Exterior / **FOOT BRIDGE** / Day

CLOSE-UP on the most hurt face.

Exterior / **LADIES' GARDEN** / Day

They turn around and start promenading the other way.

> **URSULA**
> *Sure, I think so.*
> *Yet tell her of it, hear what she will say.*
> **HERO**
> *No. Rather I will go to Benedick*
> *And counsel him to fight against his passion.*
> **URSULA**
> *O, do not do your cousin such a wrong.*
> *She cannot be so much without true judgment,*
> *Having so swift and excellent a wit*
> *As she is prized to have, as to refuse*
> *So rare a gentleman as Signior Benedick.*
> **HERO**
> *He is the only man of Italy,*
> *Always excepted my dear Claudio.*

They laugh together.

> **URSULA**
> *When are you married, madam?*
> **HERO**
> *Why, every day...tomorrow!*

They turn to look at BEATRICE.

> **URSULA** [Whispered]
> *She's limed, I warrant you. We*
> *have caught her, madam.*
> **HERO**
> *If it prove so, then loving goes by haps.*
> *Some Cupid kills with arrows, some with traps.*

They run to the house, and we see BEATRICE emerge very slowly from the cluster of trees. She moves towards the swing; it is almost sunset.

Exterior / **SWING** / Sunset

We track with her and move very close on a very quiet, much moved BEATRICE.

> **BEATRICE**
> *What fire is in mine ears? Can this be true?*
> *Stand I condemned for pride and scorn so much?*
> *Contempt, farewell; and maiden pride, adieu.*

No glory lives behind the back of such.

She sits on the swing.

> *And, Benedick, love on. I will requite thee,*
> *Taming my wild heart to thy loving hand.*
> *If thou dost love, my kindness shall incite thee*
> *To bind our loves up in a holy band.*
> *For others say thou dost deserve, and I*
> *Believe it better than reportingly.*

She begins to swing, and laugh, and cry. As the sunset takes full magical hold, we begin a series of beautiful dissolves. The music, perhaps a reprise of 'Sigh No More, Ladies,' swells to romantic pitch and these intercut shots are partly in SLOW MOTION. DISSOLVE.

Exterior / **FOUNTAIN** / Sunset
SLOW TRACK around the splashing form of BENEDICK playing and laughing in SLOW MOTION. DISSOLVE.

Exterior / **SWING** / Sunset
SLOW TRACK around the most fairyish bower, in which BEATRICE beatifically swings. DISSOLVE.

Exterior / **FOUNTAIN** / Sunset
CLOSE through the water on BENEDICK'S happiness.

Exterior / **SWING** / Sunset
Ditto BEATRICE's ecstatic face. DISSOLVE.

Exterior / **WASH HOUSE ROAD** / Night
From out of a mad dark night come galloping on imaginary horses two comic psychopaths: the physical malaprops, taking with utter seriousness their role as Cassidy and Sundance of the local constabulary. We PAN along the troupe that make up THE WATCH, who are of assorted height, face, and intellectual capacity. Their dress is a mixture of efficient police uniform and character coziness. The Three Stooges meet *Terminator II.* DOGBERRY is now ready to inspect and instruct his men before their nighttime vigil. He steps out of the line. This is Patton talking to the troops.

> **DOGBERRY**
> *Are you good men and true?*
> **ALL**
> *Yea!*

DOGBERRY
Being chosen for the prince's Watch.
This is your charge: You are to bid any man
stand, in the prince's name.
FRANCES SEACOLE
How if a' will not stand?
DOGBERRY
Why, then, take no note of him, but let him go.

He is intent, serious. Daring any one to correct him. VERGES nervously backs up his infallible chief.

VERGES
If he will not stand when he is bidden, he is
none of the prince's subjects.

DOGBERRY jumps on this as if delivering the secret of life itself.

DOGBERRY
True! and they are to meddle with none but
the prince's subjects.

Thrilled with that remark, he continues his sergeant-major speech.

DOGBERRY
You shall also make no noise in the streets.

There is a muffled cough.

GEORGE SEACOLE
We will rather sleep than talk.
DOGBERRY
Why, you speak like an ancient and most quiet
watchman, for I cannot see how sleeping should
offend.

Now into the big stuff.

DOGBERRY
If you meet a thief you may suspect him, by
virtue of your office, to be no true man; and
for such kind of men, the less you meddle or
make with them, why, the more is for your honesty.
VERGES
You have been always called a merciful man, partner.
DOGBERRY [Touched]
Truly, I would not hang a dog by my will, much

more a man who hath any honesty in him.
VERGES
'Tis very true.
DOGBERRY
Well, masters, good night. An there
be any matter of weight chances, call up me.
[TO VERGES] *Come, neighbour.*
FRANCES SEACOLE
We hear our charge.
GEORGE SEACOLE
Let us go sit here upon the bench till two, and
then all to bed.

THE WATCH take their places on the steps of the wash house and settle in for the night. Relief all round is silenced as a familiar VOICE booms out of the black.

DOGBERRY
One word more, honest neighbours. I pray you,
watch about Signior Leonato's door, for the
wedding being there tomorrow, there is a great
coil tonight. Adieu. Be vigitant, I beseech you.

DOGBERRY and VERGES go.

Exterior Night / **PAN ACROSS THE DINNER TABLE**

Supper on the Great Wedding's eve. We PAN along this jolliest of households to find a devoted HERO and CLAUDIO, eyes locked together in joy, unaware as we CUT to a terrifying electric storm roaring itself into the night. CUT.

Interior / **LEONATO'S VILLA WINE CELLARS** / Dawn

Cavernous underground wine vaults. BORACHIO and DON JOHN scurry through the tunnel-like cellars. There are huge casks, hanging cheeses, salamis. The angry men grab and chew bits of food during the scene.

DON JOHN
It is so: the Count Claudio shall marry the
daughter of Leonato.
BORACHIO
Yea, my lord, but I can cross it.
DON JOHN
Any bar, any cross, any impediment will be
medicinable to me. I am sick in displeasure to
him, and whatsoever comes athwart his affection

ranges evenly with mine. How canst thou cross this
marriage?
BORACHIO
Not honestly, my lord, but so covertly that no
dishonesty shall appear in me.
DON JOHN
Show me briefly how!
BORACHIO
I think I told your lordship a year since how
much I am in the favour of Margaret, the
waiting gentlewoman to Hero.
DON JOHN
I remember.
BORACHIO
I can at any unseasonable instant of the night
appoint her to look out at her lady's chamber
window.
DON JOHN
What life is in that to be the death of this marriage?
BORACHIO [With relish]
The poison of that lies in you to temper.
[DISSOLVE]

Exterior / **VILLA** / Night

Interior / **BENEDICK'S ROOM** / Night
Very late. The night before the wedding. In a large mirror we see
a love-sick BENEDICK sucking in his cheeks and choosing a silk
scarf from a vast array, arranged like ties next to each other on
a stand.

Interior / **UPSTAIRS CORRIDOR** / Night
DON PEDRO, CLAUDIO, LEONATO, and ANTONIO reach the open door. They
burst out laughing.

> **BENEDICK** [Appalled]
> *Gallants, I am not as I have been.*
> **LEONATO**
> *So say I. Me thinks you are sadder.*
> **CLAUDIO**
> *I hope he be in love.*

BENEDICK walks to the group at the door and talks directly to LEONATO.

> **BENEDICK**
> *Old signior, walk aside with me. I have studied*

eight or nine wise words to speak to you which
these hobby - horses must not hear.

The men continue to stifle their laughter as BENEDICK leads them off
down the corridor.

> **DON PEDRO** [*Delighted*]
> *For my life, to break with him about Beatrice.*

Interior / **UPSTAIRS CORRIDOR** / Night

Noiselessly DON JOHN has appeared behind them, and his sinisterly
whispered first line startles DON PEDRO and CLAUDIO.

> **DON JOHN**
> *My lord, and brother, God save you.*

DON PEDRO answers tentatively. His brother's face is
completely grim.

> **DON PEDRO**
> *Good e'en, brother.*
> **DON JOHN**
> *If your leisure served, I would speak with you.*

This is clearly very serious.

> **DON PEDRO**
> *In private?*
> **DON JOHN**
> *If it please you. Yet Count Claudio may hear,*
> *for what I would speak of concerns him.*

They draw aside into BENEDICK'S room and speak in
urgent whispers.

> **DON PEDRO**
> *What's the matter?*
> **DON JOHN**
> *You may think I love you not; let that appear*
> *hereafter, and aim better at me by that I now*
> *will manifest.*
> [*To* CLAUDIO]
> *Means your lordship to be married tomorrow?*
> **DON PEDRO** [*Impatient*]
> *You know he does.*

The camera moves slowly past DON JOHN and onto the increasingly
troubled face of CLAUDIO.

DON JOHN
I know not that when he knows what I know.
[Dissolve]

Exterior / **BALCONY** / Night

Borachio and Margaret begin to make love. Cut.

Exterior / **INNER COURTYARD/WELL** / Night

Don John, Don Pedro, and Claudio's point of view. In silhouette, we can see Borachio and Margaret making love. Claudio lets out a cry and makes to run at them but is held by Don Pedro and Don John. All three are shaking.

DON JOHN [*Intense, emotional*]
The lady is disloyal!
If you love her, then, tomorrow wed her. But it
would better fit your honour to change your
mind.

Close on Claudio. Tears in angry eyes. Dissolve.

Interior / **HERO'S BEDCHAMBER** / Night

Hero, blissfully unaware, lies peacefully asleep.

Exterior / **WASH HOUSE ROAD** / Night

The sleeping Watch hear a noise.

BORACHIO
What, Conrade!

The Watch all scurry behind the Wash House Pillars, smother their lanterns, and crouch behind the enormous structure. Borachio comes into view with Conrade just behind, although the drunken Borachio is unaware.

BORACHIO
Conrade, I say.
CONRADE [*Tapping him on the shoulder*]
Here, man, I am at thy elbow.
BORACHIO
Mass, an my elbow itched, I thought there
would a scab follow.
CONRADE
I will owe thee an answer for that. And now,
forward with thy tale.
BORACHIO [*Sitting on the steps*]
Sit close, then.

Exterior / **WASH HOUSE PILLARS** / Night

> **FRANCES SEACOLE** [*Whispered*]
> *Some treason, masters.*
> **HUGH OATCAKE**
> *I know him.*

Exterior / **WASH HOUSE** / Night

A slow smile breaks on BORACHIO's face. He takes a drink from a bottle he has with him. He is barely able to contain his delight.

> **BORACHIO**
> *I have tonight wooed Margaret, the Lady Hero's*
> *gentlewoman, by the name of Hero. I should first*
> *tell thee how the prince, Claudio, and my*
> *master, planted by my master, Don John, saw this*
> *'amiable' encounter.*
> **CONRADE**
> *And thought they Margaret was Hero?*

Cut to CLOSE on THE WATCH's horrified faces.

> **BORACHIO**
> *Yea and away went Claudio enraged…*

THE WATCH move as one man.

Exterior / **WASH HOUSE ROAD** / Night

> **FRANCES SEACOLE**
> *We charge you in the prince's name. Stand.*

THE WATCH surround the terrified pair and circle them menacingly with ropes and weapons at the ready.

> **HUGH OATCAKE**
> *Call up the right Master Constable. We*
> *have here recovered the most dangerous piece of*
> *lechery that ever was known in the commonwealth.*
> **CONRADE**
> *Masters, masters!*
> **GEORGE SEACOLE** [*Threatening*]
> *Never speak.*
> [DISSOLVE]

Exterior / **INNER COURTYARD** / Day

We CRANE down from the Upper Loggia as the women start to tear around the rooms within. We reach the main doors as an ultra-agitated LEONATO emerges, still in nightshirt, to greet DOGBERRY and

VERGES, who have begged for this urgent meeting with the master of the house. LEONATO stands at his front door, shivering.

> **LEONATO**
> *What would you with me, honest neighbour?*
> **VERGES**
> *Marry, sir, our watch tonight, excepting your*
> *worship's presence, ha' ta'en a couple of as*
> *arrant knaves as any in Messina.*

Garrulous apologies flood out from DOGBERRY. DOGBERRY talks to VERGES as if he's deaf.

> **DOGBERRY** [To LEONATO]
> *A good old man, sir. He will be talking. As*
> *they say, when the age is in, the wit is out.* [To VERGES]
> *Well said, i' faith, neighbour Verges.* [To LEONATO]
> *Well, God's a good man. An two men ride of*
> *a horse, one must ride behind.* [To VERGES]
> *All men are not alike, alas, good neighbour.*
> **LEONATO** [Dryly]
> *Indeed, neighbour, he comes too short*
> *of you.*
> **DOGBERRY** [Quiet pride]
> *Gifts that God gives!*
> **LEONATO**
> *Neighbours, you are tedious.*
> **DOGBERRY** [Very moved by this]
> *It pleases your worship to say so, but we are*
> *the poor duke's officers. But truly, for mine*
> *own part, if I were as tedious as a king, I could*
> *find in my heart to bestow it all of your*
> *worship.*
> **LEONATO** [Completely nonplussed]
> *All thy tediousness on me?*
> [Shaking his head] *Ah.*
> [Now he knows they are mad]
> *I would fain know what you have to say!*
> **DOGBERRY**
> *Our watch, sir, have indeed*
> *comprehended two auspicious persons, and we*
> *would have them this morning examined before*
> *your worship.*
> **LEONATO**
> *Take their examination yourself, and bring*
> *it me. I am now in great haste, as it*

may appear unto you.
Drink some wine ere you go. [He goes]
DOGBERRY [*Very self-important*]
We are now to examination these men.

He looks to VERGES and then gives the full John Wayne.

DOGBERRY
Meet me at the jail. [Dissolve]

Exterior / **CHAPEL YARD** / Day
A crowd of 100 are gathered in front of the small, chapel-sized
church, which is on the grounds of the house. The whole place is
bedecked with flowers. LEONATO, THE FRIAR, and the radiant HERO
emerge from the house and take their wedding march towards the
chapel accompanied by great applause. We CRANE up as they come
towards us and then follow them through the congregation.

DON PEDRO and CLAUDIO wait at the front of the crowd next to a
makeshift outdoor table/altar. BEATRICE and BENEDICK are at the front
also, on the bride's and groom's side, respectively. The
crowd quietens.

THE FRIAR moves towards the couple.

FRIAR
You come hither, my lord, to marry this lady.
CLAUDIO
No.
LEONATO [*Nervous laughter*]
To be married to her, you
come to marry her.

THE FRIAR smiles, the crowd relaxes.

FRIAR
Lady, you come hither to be married to this count.
HERO
I do.
FRIAR
If either of you know any inward impediment why
you should not be conjoined, I charge you, on
your souls, to utter it.
CLAUDIO
Know you any, Hero?
HERO
None, my lord.
FRIAR [*Slightly perplexed*]
Know you any, count?

Leonato [Eager]
I dare make his answer, none.
Claudio
Stand thee by, friar. Father, by your leave;
Will you with free and unconstrained soul
Give me this maid, your daughter?
Leonato [Proudly]
As freely, son, as God did give her me.

He takes Hero's hand and places it in Claudio's.

Claudio
And what have I to give you back, whose worth
May counterpoise this rich and precious gift?
Don Pedro [Firmly]
Nothing, unless you render her again.
Claudio
Sweet prince, you learn me noble thankfulness.

Then, with great venom,

Claudio
There, Leonato, take her back again.

He throws her to the ground. Beatrice rushes to her cousin's side. In a moment, chaos has come. Leonato is signalling to people to cool down, but the enraged Claudio continues.

Claudio
Give not this rotten orange to your friend;
She's but the sign and semblance of her honour.
Behold how like a maid she blushes here!
Would you not swear,
All you that see her, that she were a maid,
By these exterior shows? But she is none;
She knows the heat of a luxurious bed.

More shrieks and outrage from The Crowd. Can this be true?

Leonato
What do you mean, my lord?
Claudio
Not to be married, [Gasps]
Not to knit my soul to an approved wanton.

Leonato, now desperately trying to gauge an unpleasant truth, begins to think on his feet, appalling though the situation is. He attempts to make this intimate unheard by the riveted Crowd.

LEONATO
Dear my lord, if you, in your own proof,
Have vanquished the resistance of her youth,
And made defeat of her virginity –
CLAUDIO [*Public, walking amongst the crowd*]
No, Leonato,
I never tempted her with word too large,
But as a brother to his sister, showed
Bashful sincerity and comely love.
HERO
And seemed I ever otherwise to you?
CLAUDIO [*Fighting tears*]
You seem to me as Dian in her orb.
But you are more intemperate in your blood
Than Venus or those pampered animals
That rage in savage sensuality.

HERO lies, almost sick, in BEATRICE's arms. BENEDICK looks
on appalled.

HERO
Is my lord well, that he doth speak so wide?
LEONATO [*Desperate*]
Sweet prince, why speak not you?
DON PEDRO [*Icy*]
What shall I speak?
I stand dishonoured that have gone about
To link my dear friend to a common stale.
CLAUDIO
What man was he talked with you yesternight
Out at your window betwixt twelve and one?
HERO [*Terrified*]
I talked with no man at that hour, my lord.
DON PEDRO [*Stepping forward*]
Why, then are you no maiden. Leonato,
I am sorry you must hear. Upon mine honour,
Myself, my brother, and this grieved count
Did see her, hear her, at that hour last night

Angle on the stunned face of MARGARET at the back of THE
CROWD. She realises everything in a second.

DON PEDRO
Talk with a ruffian at her chamber window;
Who hath indeed, most like a liberal villain,
Confessed the vile encounters they have had

A thousand times in secret.

THE CROWD is stunned. Reactions of BEATRICE, BENEDICK. LEONATO is
beaten. HERO faints once more.

THE CROWD react as if this is some proof. DON JOHN acts quickly.

> **DON JOHN**
> *Come, let us go. These things, come thus to light,*
> *Smother her spirits up.*

The princes and the count leave. THE CROWD likewise starts to
move away.

> **LEONATO** [*Grimly, to himself*]
> *Hath no man's dagger here a point for me?*

We CUT.

Exterior / **CHAPEL YARD** / Day

Top shot showing the debris as THE CROWD disperses. Furniture is
overturned, flowers are strewn. A bleak, tiny group, LEONATO,
ANTONIO, BEATRICE, URSULA, THE FRIAR, BENEDICK, gather around the
hapless HERO, whose wedding day has turned into a nightmare. HERO
starts to come to. LEONATO grabs her by the hair, exploding
with rage.

> **LEONATO**
> *Do not live, Hero, do not ope thine eyes,*
> *Grieved I, I had but one? Why had I one?*
> *Why ever wast thou lovely in my eyes?*
> *She, O, she is fallen*
> *Into a pit of ink.*
> **BENEDICK**
> *Sir, sir, be patient.*
> *For my part, I am so attired in wonder*
> *I know not what to say.*
> **BEATRICE**
> *O, on my soul, my cousin is belied!*
> **BENEDICK**
> *Lady, were you her bedfellow last night?*
> **BEATRICE**
> *No, truly not; although until last night*
> *I have this twelvemonth been her bedfellow.*
> **LEONATO**
> *Confirmed, confirmed.*
> *Would the two princes lie and Claudio lie?*
> *Hence from her, let her die.*

LEONATO weeps quietly as does HERO, as does BEATRICE. The atmosphere is desperately sad, but calmer. THE FRIAR takes his opportunity.

> **FRIAR**
> *Hear me a little;*
> *Lady, what man is he you are accused of?*
> **HERO**
> *They know that do accuse me. I know none.*
> **FRIAR**
> *There is some strange misprision in the princes.*
> **BENEDICK**
> *Two of them have the very bent of honour;*
> *And if their wisdoms be misled in this,*
> *The practice of it lives in John the Bastard.*

Suddenly we begin to see a little of the LEONATO of old.

> **LEONATO**
> *If they wrong her honour,*
> *The proudest of them shall well hear of it.*

Sanity is beginning to return.

> **FRIAR**
> *Pause awhile,*
> *And let my counsel sway you in this case.*
> *Your daughter here the princes left for dead,*
> *Let her a while be secretly kept in,*
> *And publish it that she is dead indeed.*
> **LEONATO**
> *What shall become of this?*
> **FRIAR**
> *She dying, as it must be so maintained,*
> *Upon the instant that she was accused,*
> *Shall be lamented, pitied, and excused*
> *Of every hearer. So will it fare with Claudio.*
> *When he shall hear she died upon his words,*
> *The idea of her life shall sweetly creep*
> *Into his study of imagination,*
> *And every lovely organ of her life*
> *Shall come apparelled in more precious habit,*
> *Than when she lived indeed. Then shall he mourn,*
> *And wish he had not so accused her.*
> **BENEDICK** [Interrupting]
> *Signior Leonato, let the friar advise you.*

LEONATO
Being that I flow in grief,
The smallest twine may lead me.
FRIAR
'Tis well consented. Presently away;

LEONATO and ANTONIO exit. HERO and URSULA and BEATRICE rise. URSULA and THE FRIAR lead her away to the house.

FRIAR
Come, lady, die to live. This wedding day
Perhaps is but prolonged. Have patience, and endure.

They go. BEATRICE rises and goes into the little chapel.

Interior / **CHAPEL** / Day

BEATRICE, her back to us, kneels at the bench nearest the door. She is hunched over and praying / attempting to control her distress. BENEDICK approaches and kneels beside her. In the background a large but simple wooden cross hangs on the wall between them.

BENEDICK
Lady Beatrice, have you wept all this while?
BEATRICE
Yea, and I will weep a while longer.
BENEDICK
I will not desire that.
BEATRICE
You have no reason, I do it freely.
BENEDICK
Surely I do believe your fair cousin is wronged.
BEATRICE
Ah, how much might the man deserve of me
that would right her!
BENEDICK
Is there any way to show such friendship?
BEATRICE
A very even way, but no such friend.
BENEDICK
May a man do it?
BEATRICE
It is a man's office, but not yours.

Beat. Then, quite simply,

BENEDICK
I do love nothing in the world so well as you.

Is not that strange?
BEATRICE [Shocked]
As strange as the thing I know not. It were as possible for me to say I loved nothing so well as you, but believe me not, and yet I lie not. I confess nothing, nor I deny nothing. I am sorry for my cousin.
BENEDICK
By my sword, Beatrice, thou lovest me.
BEATRICE
Do not swear and eat it.
BENEDICK
I will swear by it that you love me, and I will make him eat it that says I love not you.
BEATRICE
Why then, God forgive me.
BENEDICK
What offence, sweet Beatrice?
BEATRICE
You have stayed me in a happy hour. I was about to protest I loved you.
BENEDICK
And do it with all thy heart.
BEATRICE
I love you with so much of my heart that none is left to protest.
BENEDICK
Come, bid me do anything for thee.
BEATRICE
Kill Claudio.
BENEDICK
Ha! Not for the wide world.
BEATRICE
You kill me to deny it. [She gets up to go] *Farewell.*
BENEDICK
Tarry, sweet Beatrice. [He stops her]
BEATRICE
I am gone though I am here. There is no love in you. Nay, I pray you, let me go.
BENEDICK
Beatrice.
BEATRICE
In faith, I will go.

BENEDICK

We'll be friends first.

BEATRICE

*You dare easier be friends with me than fight
with mine enemy.*

BENEDICK

Is Claudio thine enemy?

BEATRICE

*Is a' not approved in the height a villain, that
hath slandered, scorned, dishonoured my
kinswoman? O that I were a man! What, bear her
in hand until they come to take hands, and then
with public accusation, uncovered slander,
unmitigated rancour – O God, that I were a man! I
would eat his heart in the market place.*

BENEDICK

Hear me, Beatrice.

BEATRICE

Talk with a man out at a window! A proper saying!

BENEDICK

Nay, but Beatrice –

BEATRICE

*Sweet Hero, she is wronged, she is slandered,
she is undone.*

BENEDICK

Beat...

BEATRICE

*He is now as valiant as Hercules that only tells
a lie and swears it. I cannot be a man with
wishing, therefore I will die a woman with grieving.*

BENEDICK

By this hand, I love thee.

BEATRICE

*Use it for my love some other way than swearing
by it.*

BENEDICK

*Think you in your soul the Count Claudio hath
wronged Hero?*

BEATRICE

Yea, as sure as I have a thought or a soul.

BENEDICK

*Enough, I am engaged, I will challenge him.
Go comfort your cousin. I must say she is dead.
And so, farewell.*

BEATRICE goes. BENEDICK looks after her, then turns as we DISSOLVE.

ESCAPE TUNNEL / Day

A maniacally laughing DON JOHN makes his escape down an apparently endless torch-lit corridor.

Interior / **PRISON** / Day

Light streaming in through barred windows to a dark, damp, dungeon-like cellar. DOGBERRY in Perry Mason mode. THE SEXTON serious, determined. The two villains sit astride poles protruding from the wall, parallel to the floor and high. Their feet are tied down to the floor, their hands to the ceiling. It is at once bizarre and extremely uncomfortable.

> **DOGBERRY**
> *Is our whole dissembly appeared?*

The business-like SEXTON interrupts him.

> **SEXTON**
> *Which be the malefactors?*
> **DOGBERRY**
> *Marry, that am I and my partner.*
> **SEXTON** [With a sigh]
> *But which are the offenders to be examined?*

DOGBERRY approaches BORACHIO with suspicion.

> **DOGBERRY**
> *What is your name, friend?*
> **BORACHIO**
> *Borachio.*
> **DOGBERRY**
> *Yours, sirrah?*
> **CONRADE**
> *I am a gentleman, sir, and my name is Conrade.*
> **DOGBERRY**
> *It is proved already that you are little
> better than false knaves. How answer you for
> yourselves?*
> **CONRADE**
> *Marry, sir, we say we are none.*
> **DOGBERRY** [Then to BORACHIO]
> *You?*
> **BORACHIO**
> *Sir, I say to you we are none.*

DOGBERRY
Have you writ down that they are none?
SEXTON [Utterly exasperated]
Master Constable, you go not the way to
examine. You must call forth the watch that are
their accusers.
DOGBERRY
Let the Watch come forth. Masters, I charge you
in the prince's name accuse these men.
FRANCES SEACOLE
This man said, sir, that Don John, the
prince's brother, was a villain.
DOGBERRY
Write down Prince John a villain.
BORACHIO
Master Constable.
DOGBERRY
Pray thee, fellow, peace. I do not like thy
look, I promise thee.
SEXTON
What heard you him say else?
GEORGE SEACOLE
Marry, that he had received a thousand ducats
of Don John for accusing the Lady Hero wrongfully.
DOGBERRY
Flat burglary, as ever was committed.
VERGES
Yea, by mass, that it is.
SEXTON
What else?
FRANCES SEACOLE
And that Count Claudio did mean upon
his words to disgrace Hero before the whole
assembly, and not marry her.
DOGBERRY [Appalled]
Thou wilt be condemned into
everlasting redemption for this.
SEXTON
What else?
GEORGE SEACOLE
This is all. [The terrible truth dawns on the SEXTON]
SEXTON
Prince John is this morning secretly stolen
away. Hero was in this manner accused, in this

very manner refused, and upon the grief of this
suddenly died. Master Constable, let these men
be bound and brought to Leonato's.
DOGBERRY
Come, let them be opinioned.
VERGES
Let them be, in the hands.
CONRADE
Off, coxcomb!
DOGBERRY
God's my life, where's the sexton? Let him
write down the prince's officer coxcomb. Come,
bind them. Thou naughty varlet!
CONRADE
Away, you are an ass, you are an ass.

DOGBERRY stops in his tracks. Dumbfounded, appalled, and instantly
bent on revenge he walks slowly and menacingly back to the already
regretful CONRADE.

DOGBERRY
Dost thou not suspect my place? [Yelling] *Dost thou*
not suspect my years?
[Looking back to where the SEXTON had been]
O that he were here to write me down an ass!
But, masters, remember that I am *an ass;*
though it be not written down, yet forget not
that I am an ass.

He is clearly just beginning as we DISSOLVE.

Exterior / **STABLES** / Day
LEONATO, visibly older, takes a grim-faced constitutional with his
worried brother. We TRACK with them as they walk.

ANTONIO
If you go on thus, you will kill yourself.
LEONATO
Bring me a father that so loved his child,
Whose joy of her is overwhelmed like mine,
And bid him speak of patience.
But there is no such man, for, brother, men
Can counsel and speak comfort to that grief
Which they themselves not feel, but tasting it,
Their counsel turns to passion.
I pray thee, peace. I will be flesh and blood;

For there was never yet philosopher
That could endure the toothache patiently.
ANTONIO
Yet bend not all the harm upon yourself.
Make those that do offend you suffer, too.
LEONATO
There thou speak'st reason, nay I will do so.
My soul doth tell me Hero is belied,
And that shall Claudio know, so shall the prince,
And all of them that thus dishonour her.
ANTONIO
Here comes the prince and Claudio hastily.

Exterior / **STABLES** / Day

DON PEDRO and CLAUDIO are determinedly walking to their horses.
They do not want to have this conversation.

DON PEDRO
Good e'en, good e'en.
CLAUDIO
Good day to both of you.
LEONATO
Hear you, my lords?
DON PEDRO
We have some haste.
LEONATO
Some haste, my lord! Well, fare you well, my lord.
Are you so hasty now? Well, all is one.

LEONATO and ANTONIO head them off.

DON PEDRO
Nay, do not quarrel with us, good old man.
ANTONIO
If he could right himself with quarrelling,
Some of us would lie low.
CLAUDIO
Who wrongs him?
LEONATO
Marry, thou dost wrong me, thou dissembler, thou.
Nay, never lay thy hand upon thy sword,
I fear thee not.
CLAUDIO
Marry, beshrew my hand
If it should give your age such cause of fear.
In faith, my hand meant nothing to my sword.

LEONATO
Tush, tush, man, never fleer and jest at me.
I speak not like a dotard nor a fool,
I say thou hast belied mine innocent child.
DON PEDRO
You say not right, old man.
LEONATO
My lord, my lord,
I'll prove it on his body if he dare.
CLAUDIO [Pushing him off]
Away, I will not have to do with you.
LEONATO
Canst thou so daff me? Thou hast killed my child.
If thou kill'st me, boy, thou shalt kill a man.
ANTONIO
He shall kill two of us, and men indeed.
But that's no matter, let him kill one first.
I'll whip you from your foining fence.
Nay, as I am a gentleman, I will.

They scuffle.

LEONATO
Brother.
ANTONIO
Content yourself. God knows, I loved my niece,
And she is dead, slandered to death by villains
Scambling, outfacing, fashion-monging boys,
That lie, and cog, and flout, deprave, and slander.
LEONATO
Brother Antony.
ANTONIO
Come, 'tis no matter,
Do not you meddle, let me deal in this.
DON PEDRO [Absolutely firm]
Gentlemen both, we will not wake your patience.
My heart is sorry for your daughter's death,
But on my honour she was charged with nothing
But what was true and very full of proof.
LEONATO
My lord, my lord.
DON PEDRO
I will not hear you.
LEONATO
No? Come brother, away. I will be heard.

ANTONIO
And shall, or some of us will smart for it.

Exterior / **STABLES** / Day

A stone-faced BENEDICK approaches on horseback.

DON PEDRO [*Relieved*]
See, see, here comes the man we went to seek.
CLAUDIO
Now signior, what news?
BENEDICK
Good day, my lord.
DON PEDRO
*Welcome, signior. You are almost come to part
almost a fray.*
CLAUDIO
*We had liked to have had our two noses snapped
off with two old men without teeth.*
BENEDICK
Shall I speak a word in your ear?

Without warning he grabs CLAUDIO roughly by the face and thrusts
him to the wall.

BENEDICK
*You are a villain. I jest not. I will make it
good how you dare, with what you dare, and when
you dare. Do me right, or I will protest your
cowardice. You have killed a sweet lady, and her
death shall fall heavy on you.*

Beat.

*Fare you well, boy, you know my mind.
My lord, for your many courtesies I thank you.
I must discontinue your company.
Your brother the bastard is fled from Messina.
You have among you killed a sweet and
innocent lady. For my Lord Lackbeard there,
he and I shall meet, and till then, peace be
with him.*

BENEDICK exits.

DON PEDRO
He is in earnest.
CLAUDIO
In most profound earnest.

DON PEDRO
And hath challenged thee.
CLAUDIO
Most sincerely.

Exterior / **STABLES** / Day

THE WATCH arrive noisily with their prisoners bound.

DON PEDRO
Officers, what offence have these men done?
DOGBERRY
Marry, sir, they have committed false report;
moreover, they have spoken untruths; secondarily,
they are slanders; sixth and lastly, they have
belied a lady; thirdly, they have verified
unjust things; and, to conclude, they are lying knaves.
DON PEDRO
Who have you offended, masters, that you are
thus bound to your answer? This learned
constable is too cunning to be understood.
BORACHIO
I have deceived even your very eyes. What
your wisdoms could not discover, these shallow
fools have brought to light, who in the night
overheard me confessing to this man how Don John
your brother incensed me to slander the Lady
Hero, how you saw me court Margaret.
How you disgraced Hero when you should marry
her. The lady is dead upon mine and my
master's false accusation.
CLAUDIO [Devastated]
Sweet Hero.
DOGBERRY
Come, bring away the plaintiffs. By this time
our sexton hath reformed Signior Leonato of the
matter. And masters, do not forget to specify,
when time and place shall serve, that I am an ass.
VERGES
Here, here comes Master Signior Leonato, and the
sexton, too.

Exterior / **STABLES** / Day

From the house come LEONATO, ANTONIO, and THE SEXTON.

LEONATO
Which is the villain? Let me see his eyes.

BORACHIO

If you would know your wronger, look on me.

LEONATO

Art thou the slave that with thy breath hast
killed mine innocent child?

BORACHIO

Yea, even I alone.

LEONATO

No, not so, villain, thou beliest thyself.
Here stand a pair of honourable men.
A third is fled that had a hand in it.
I thank you, princes, for my daughter's death.
Record it with your high and worthy deeds.
'Twas bravely done, if you bethink you of it.

CLAUDIO

I know not how to pray your patience,
Yet I must speak. Choose your revenge yourself,
Impose me to what penance your invention
Can lay upon my sin. Yet sinned I not
But in mistaking.

DON PEDRO

By my soul, nor I.

LEONATO [Gravely]

I cannot bid you bid my daughter live;
That were impossible: but I pray you both
Possess the people in Messina here
How innocent she died, and if your love
Can labour aught in sad invention,
Hang her an epitaph upon her tomb
And sing it to her bones, sing it tonight.
Tomorrow morning come you to my house,
And since you could not be my son-in-law,
Be yet my nephew. My brother hath a daughter,
Almost the copy of my child that's dead,
And she alone is heir to both of us.
Give her the right you should have giv'n her cousin,
And so dies my revenge.

CLAUDIO

O noble sir!
Your overkindness doth wring tears from me.
I do embrace your offer; and dispose
For henceforth of poor Claudio.

LEONATO

Tomorrow then I will expect your coming.

Tonight I take my leave. This naughty man
Shall face to face be brought to Margaret,
Who I believe was packed in all this wrong.
BORACHIO
No, by my soul, she was not,
Nor knew not what she did when she spoke to me,
But always hath been just and virtuous
In anything that I do know by her.
DOGBERRY
Moreover, sir, which indeed is not
under white and black, this plaintiff here, the
offender, did call me ass. I beseech you, let it
be remembered in his punishment.
LEONATO
I thank thee for thy care and honest pains.
DOGBERRY
Your worship speaks like a most thankful and
reverend youth, and I praise God for you.
LEONATO
There's for thy pains.
DOGBERRY
God save the foundation.
LEONATO
Go. I discharge thee of thy prisoner, and I
thank thee.
DOGBERRY
I leave with your worship an arrant knave,
which I beseech your worship to correct
yourself, for the example of others. God
restore you to health. I humbly give you leave
to depart, and if a merry meeting may
be wished, God prohibit it. Come, neighbour.

Exeunt THE MAD HORSEMEN.

LEONATO
Until tomorrow morning, lords, farewell.
ANTONIO
Farewell, my lords. We look for you tomorrow.
DON PEDRO
We will not fail.
CLAUDIO
Tonight I'll mourn with Hero.

As they move back towards the house, we DISSOLVE.

Exterior / **MOUNTAIN TOP** / Night

Point of view from the Villa of a wide shot of a cloaked, torched procession towards HERO'S tomb. Beautiful and sombre, a snake of lights against the hillside. We pull back to reveal ANTONIO and HERO in the foreground. We move closer to the procession and see DON PEDRO, CLAUDIO, and a choir of mourners sing as CLAUDIO weeps before the tomb.

CLAUDIO
Done to death by slanderous tongues
Was the Hero that here lies.
Death in guerdon of her wrongs
Gives her fame which never dies.
So the life that died with shame
Lives in death with glorious fame.
[Hangs up the scroll]

BALTHASAR [Sings]
Pardon, goddess of the night,
Those that slew thy virgin knight,
For the which with songs of woe
Round about her tomb they go.
Midnight, assist our moan,
Help us to sigh and groan,
Heavily, heavily.
Graves yawn, and yield your dead
Till death be uttered,
Heavily, heavily. [Dissolve]

Exterior / **VILLA** / Morning

Exterior / **LOVERS' BOWER** / Dawn

BENEDICK awaits the arrival of BEATRICE. He has written a song, which (alas) he's attempting to practise.

BENEDICK
The god of love,
That sits above,
And knows me, and knows me,
How pitiful I deserve –
[To camera] *I mean in singing; but in loving,*
Leander the good swimmer, Troilus the first
employer of panders, and a whole book full of
these quondam carpet-mongers, whose names yet
run smoothly in the even road of a blank verse,
why, they were never so truly turned over and
over as my poor self in love. Marry, I cannot

*show it in rhyme. I have tried. I can find out
no rhyme to 'lady' but 'baby,' an innocent
rhyme; for 'scorn,' 'horn,' a hard rhyme; for
'school' 'fool,' a babbling rhyme. Very ominous
endings. No, I was not born under a rhyming
planet, nor I cannot woo in festival terms.*

Suddenly BEATRICE is there.

BENEDICK [*Genuinely surprised*]
Sweet Beatrice, wouldst thou come when I called thee?
BEATRICE
Yea, signior, and depart when you bid me.
BENEDICK
O, stay but till then.
BEATRICE
'Then' is spoken. Fare you well now.

She *almost* goes but then sits in the bower seat. He sits next to her.
Very close.

BEATRICE
*And yet ere I go, let me go with that I came
for, which is with knowing what hath passed
between you and Claudio.*
BENEDICK
Only foul words, and thereupon I will kiss thee.
BEATRICE
*Foul words is but foul wind, and foul wind is
but foul breath, and foul breath is noisome,
therefore I will depart unkissed.*
BENEDICK
*Thou hast frighted the word out of his right
sense, so forcible is thy wit. But I must tell
thee plainly, Claudio undergoes my challenge,
and either I must shortly hear from him or I
will subscribe him a coward. And I pray thee now
tell me, for which of my bad parts didst thou
first fall in love with me?*
BEATRICE
*For them all together, which maintain so
politic a state of evil that they will not admit
any good part to intermingle with them. But for
which of my good parts did you first suffer love
for me?*

BENEDICK

*Suffer love! A good epithet. I do suffer love
indeed, for I love thee against my will.*

BEATRICE

*In spite of your heart, I think. Alas, poor
heart. If you spite it for my sake, I will
spite it for yours, for I will never love that
which my friend hates.*

BENEDICK

*Thou and I are too wise to woo peaceably.
And now tell me, how doth your cousin?*

BEATRICE

Very ill.

BENEDICK

And how do you?

BEATRICE

Very ill too.

BENEDICK

*Serve God, love me, and mend.
Here comes one in haste.*

URSULA runs in, wildly excited.

URSULA

*Madam, you must come to your uncle. Yonder's
old coil at home. It is proved my Lady Hero hath
been falsely accused, the prince and Claudio
mightily abused, and Don John is the author of
all, who is fled and gone. Will you come presently?*

BEATRICE

Will you go hear this news, signior?

BENEDICK

*I will live in thy heart, die in thy lap, and be
buried in thy eyes. And moreover, I will go with
thee to thy uncle's.*

Exterior / **CHAPEL YARD** / Day

Enter LEONATO, BENEDICK, BEATRICE, MARGARET, URSULA, ANTONIO, THE
FRIAR, HERO, and all our regulars all pouring out of the house. An
atmosphere of wild excitement.

FRIAR

Did I not tell you she was innocent?

LEONATO

*So are the prince and Claudio who accused her
Upon the error that you heard debated.*

But Margaret was in some fault for this.
ANTONIO
Well, I am glad that all things sort so well.
LEONATO
Well, daughter, and you gentlewomen all,
Withdraw,
And when I send for you, come hither masked.

They all go back into the church.

LEONATO
The prince and Claudio promised by this hour
To visit me. You know your office, brother,
You must be father to your brother's daughter,
And give her to young Claudio.
ANTONIO
Which I will do with confirmed countenance.
BENEDICK [Aside]
Friar, I must entreat your pains, I think.
FRIAR
To do what, signior?
BENEDICK
To bind me or undo me, one of them.
Signior Leonato, truth it is, good signior,
Your niece regards me with an eye of favour.
LEONATO
The sight whereof I think you had from me,
From Claudio and the prince. But what's your will?
BENEDICK
Your answer, sir, is enigmatical.
But for my will, my will is your good will
May stand with ours, this day to be conjoined
In the state of honourable marriage,
In which, good friar, I shall desire your help.
LEONATO
My heart is with your liking.
FRIAR
And my help.
Here comes the prince and Claudio.

Enter DON PEDRO and CLAUDIO and two or three others.

DON PEDRO
Good morrow to this fair assembly.
LEONATO
Good morrow, prince. Good morrow, Claudio.

We here attend you. Are you yet determined
Today to marry with my brother's daughter?

CLAUDIO nods.

LEONATO
Call her forth, brother, here's the friar ready.

ANTONIO steps into the church, and immediately the veiled women
come out. A CROWD has begun to gather at the door to the house.

CLAUDIO
Which is the lady I must seize upon?
ANTONIO
This same is she, and I do give you her.

HERO steps forward, still veiled.

CLAUDIO
Sweet, let me see your face.
LEONATO
No, that you shall not till you take her hand
Before this friar and swear to marry her.
CLAUDIO
Give me your hand before this holy friar.
I am your husband if you like of me.

As HERO removes the veil, THE CROWD gasps.

DON PEDRO [Awed]
Hero that is dead.
LEONATO [Gently]
She died, my lord, but whiles her
slander lived.
HERO
And when I lived, I was your other wife;
And when you loved, you were my other husband.
One Hero died defiled, but I do live,
And surely as I live, I am a maid.

CLOSE on the faces of the amazed lovers and the watching principals.
After a moment THE CROWD ah's and then applauds. THE FRIAR tops it.

FRIAR
All this amazement can I qualify;
When after that the holy rites are ended,
I'll tell you largely of fair Hero's death.

THE CROWD becomes boisterous and starts to make for the house.
BENEDICK stops them. The following scene is completely and

uncomfortably public.

BENEDICK [*Panicked*]
Soft and fair, friar. Which is Beatrice?
BEATRICE [*Unmasking*]
I answer to that name, what
is your will?
BENEDICK
Do not you love me?
BEATRICE
Why no, no more than reason.
BENEDICK
Why then, your uncle and the prince and Claudio
Have been deceived. They swore you did.
BEATRICE
Do not you love me?
BENEDICK
Troth no, no more than reason.
BEATRICE
Why then, my cousin, Margaret, and Ursula
Are much deceived, for they did swear you did.
BENEDICK
They swore that you were almost sick for me.
BEATRICE
They swore that you were well-nigh dead for me.
BENEDICK
'Tis no such matter. Then you do not love me?
BEATRICE
No, truly, but in friendly recompense.
LEONATO
Come, cousin, I am sure you love the gentleman.
CLAUDIO
And I'll be sworn upon 't that he loves her,

He steals a letter from BENEDICK's pocket. THE CROWD roar as they have done throughout the scene.

CLAUDIO
For here's a paper written in his hand,
A halting sonnet of his own pure brain,
Fashioned to Beatrice.
HERO
And here's another,

She steals a letter from BEATRICE's pocket.

HERO
Writ in my cousin's hand, stol'n from her pocket,
Containing her affection unto Benedick.
BENEDICK
A miracle! Here's our own hands against our
hearts. Come, I will have thee, but by this
light, I take thee for pity.
BEATRICE
I would not deny you, but by this good day, I
yield upon great persuasion, and partly to save
your life, for I was told you were in a
consumption.
BENEDICK
Peace, I will stop your mouth.

Kisses her, with the greatest tenderness. Great applause, ah's and ooo's.

DON PEDRO
How dost thou, Benedick the married man?
BENEDICK
I'll tell thee what, prince: a college of wit-
crackers cannot flout me out of my humour. Dost
thou think I care for a satire or an epigram?
No, since I do purpose to marry, I will think
nothing to any purpose that the world can say
against it, and therefore never flout at me for
what I have said against it. For man is a giddy
thing, and this is my conclusion. For thy part,
Claudio, I did think to have beaten thee, but in
that thou art like to be my kinsman, live
unbruised, and love my cousin.

CLOSE on CLAUDIO'S reaction.

BENEDICK
Come, come, we are friends, let's have a dance
ere we are married, that we may lighten our own
hearts and our wives' heels.

THE CROWD cheers.

LEONATO [Vainly]
We'll have dancing afterward.
BENEDICK
First, of my word. Therefore play, music.
Prince, thou art sad, get thee a wife!

Get thee a wife!

Exterior / **COURTYARD** / Day

A horseman rides up to the edge of the CHAPEL YARD. Behind him another group with a trussed DON JOHN. The two brothers exchange a long, terrible look. We see the reactions of each of the others, considering for a moment what might have been.

> **MESSENGER**
> *My lord, your brother John is ta'en in flight,*
> *And brought with armed men back to Messina.*

DON PEDRO, much shaken, is gently brought out of his reverie by BENEDICK, who ushers the men away.

> **BENEDICK**
> *Think not on him till tomorrow, I'll devise thee*
> *brave punishments for him. Strike up, pipers.*

As the music starts (one final reprise of 'Sigh No More'), the camera moves back and begins to rise. All the couples dance and sing merrily in front of us, and we see one joyous image of each of them. We note the melancholic, solitary figure of DON PEDRO. We carry on from the Chapel Yard, in through the house, led by the two pairs of lovers, through the inner courtyard where confetti rains down on all; out onto the Terrace, through the Formal Garden, up into the Orchard Alley, and then quickly, high into the air where we leave the people and the dancing to rise above the house, catch the late afternoon sun, the sound of happiness floating on the air, and a breathtaking view of fairy tale countryside, which allows us to FREEZE and happily DISSOLVE to BLACK.

The End

The cast

LEONATO Richard Briers

The head of the household, a wealthy and well-respected widower.
Hero is his only daughter. Beatrice, his niece, lives with him
as his ward.

BEATRICE Emma Thompson (left)

Leonato's niece. Her beauty, wit, and independent spirit make her a formidable match – in more than one sense. By the customs of the time, she is in danger of being left unmarried, but what man could rise to the challenge?

BENEDICK Kenneth Branagh (right)

A friend and confidant of Don Pedro and Claudio. As brilliant a satirist (and as fond of his own wit) as Beatrice.

CLAUDIO Robert Sean Leonard (left)

A young Florentine, who has shown himself to be valorous and loyal in Don Pedro's service. He met Hero before the campaign and fell in love with her, but now that the time has come to woo her, he feels that his inexperience puts him at a disadvantage.

HERO Kate Beckinsale (right)

Leonato's daughter – if there were other children, we never hear of them, and she is now his only heir. She has just reached marriageable age.

DON PEDRO OF ARAGON Denzel Washington

He has just led his troops to fight in a war, where they have acquitted themselves honourably. Honour is one of his preoccupations, and he is anxious to protect his own reputation and that of his friends.

DON JOHN Keanu Reeves (centre)

The bastard brother of Don Pedro, and a malcontent. Although before now he has taken sides against Don Pedro, he is now reconciled with him, but Don Pedro's generosity irks Don John, and he is especially galled by the favours shown to Claudio.

CONRADE & BORACHIO Richard Clifford (left) and Gerard Horan (right)

Aides to Don John, who share his taste for villainy.

DOGBERRY Michael Keaton (left)

The Constable of the Watch: he has an overwhelming sense of the dignity and power of his office, and an instinctive desire to avoid trouble. He sees himself as a man of action and deep investigative skills, and never fails to make sure he gets whatever credit is due to him – even if he is not *quite* clear as to what everything means or what is going on.

VERGES Ben Elton (right)

Dogberry's deputy: proud and happy to serve under his 'partner'– and to share in his delusions of grandeur (and efficiency). Watson to a village Holmes (if not Tonto to a Messinian Lone Ranger...).

FRIAR FRANCIS Jimmy Yuill

A Franciscan friar, effectively a chaplain to the household.

ANTONIO Brian Blessed

Leonato's brother. His considerable energies are directed to running the estate, which he does with great relish. He is fiercely proud of his family and protective of its honour.

MARGARET & URSULA Imelda Staunton (left)
and Phyllida Law (right)

Ladies' maids to the women of the household, and very much their
confidantes. Both enthusiastically join in the practical joking that is
going on – but Margaret's prank has sinister consequences she
was not aware of.

THE WATCH GEORGE SEACOLE Andy Hockley (left),
HUGH OATCAKE Conrad Nelson (centre), and
FRANCES SEACOLE Chris Barnes (right)

Servants and estate workers who can confidently turn their hand
to anything (including music making) and who have been recruited
into the haphazard volunteer police force.

BALTHASAR Patrick Doyle

One of Don Pedro's officers, and the regular provider of musical entertainment for him and his entourage.

MESSENGER
Alex Lowe

SEXTON
Edward Jewesbury

The film

Road and sky and heat haze.
All we can hear is the drumming of hooves.

LEONATO
*I learn in this letter that Don Pedro of
Arragon comes this night to Messina.*

DON PEDRO
*Good Signior Leonato, are you come to meet
your trouble? The fashion of the world is to
avoid cost, and you encounter it.*
LEONATO
*Never came trouble to my house
in the likeness of your grace.*

LEONATO
*Let me bid you welcome, my lord: being
reconciled to the prince your brother, I owe
you all duty.*
DON JOHN
*I thank you.
I am not of many words, but I thank you.*

BEATRICE

How tartly that gentleman looks! I never can see him but I am heart-burned an hour after.

DON JOHN
Any bar, any cross, any impediment will be medicinable to me. I am sick in displeasure to him, and whatsoever comes athwart his affection ranges evenly with mine.

DON PEDRO
*Come hither, Leonato. What
was it you told me of today, that your niece
Beatrice was* in love *with Signior Benedick?*
CLAUDIO
*I did never think that lady would have
loved any man.*
LEONATO
*No, nor I neither. But most wonderful that she
should so dote on Signior Benedick, whom she
hath in all outward behaviours seemed ever to abhor.*

HERO
They did entreat me to acquaint her of it,
But I persuaded them, if they loved Benedick,
To wish him wrestle with affection
And never to let Beatrice know of it.
URSULA
Why did you so? Doth not the gentleman
Deserve as full as fortunate a bed
As ever Beatrice shall couch upon?
HERO
O god of love! I know he doth deserve
As much as may be yielded to a man.
But nature never framed a woman's heart
Of prouder stuff than that of Beatrice.

BEATRICE

What fire is in mine ears? Can this be true?
Stand I condemned for pride and scorn so much?
Contempt, farewell; and maiden pride, adieu.
No glory lives behind the back of such.
And, Benedick, love on. I will requite thee,
Taming my wild heart to thy loving hand.

CLAUDIO
Give not this rotten orange to your friend;
She's but the sign and semblance of her honour.
Behold how like a maid she blushes here!
Would you not swear,
All you that see her, that she were a maid,
By these exterior shows? But she is none;
She knows the heat of a luxurious bed.

BENEDICK
What offence, sweet Beatrice?
BEATRICE
You have stayed me in a happy hour. I was
about to protest I loved you.
BENEDICK
And do it with all thy heart.
BEATRICE
I love you with so much of my heart that none
is left to protest.
BENEDICK
Come, bid me do anything for thee.
BEATRICE
Kill Claudio.

DOGBERRY
*Thou wilt be condemned into
everlasting redemption for this.*

CONRADE
Away, you are an ass, you are an ass.
DOGBERRY
*Dost thou not suspect my place? Dost thou
not suspect my years?
O that he were here to write me down an ass!
But, masters, remember that I am an ass;
though it be not written down, yet forget not
that I am an ass.*

CLAUDIO

I know not how to pray your patience,
Yet I must speak. Choose your revenge yourself,
Impose me to what penance your invention
Can lay upon my sin. Yet sinned I not
But in mistaking.

CLAUDIO

Done to death by slanderous tongues
Was the Hero that here lies.
Death in guerdon of her wrongs
Gives her fame which never dies.
So the life that died with shame
Lives in death with glorious fame.

DON PEDRO
How dost thou, Benedick the married man?
BENEDICK
*I'll tell thee what, prince: a college of wit-
crackers cannot flout me out of my humour.*

BENEDICK
Come, come, we are friends, let's have a dance
ere we are married, that we may lighten our own
hearts and our wives' heels.

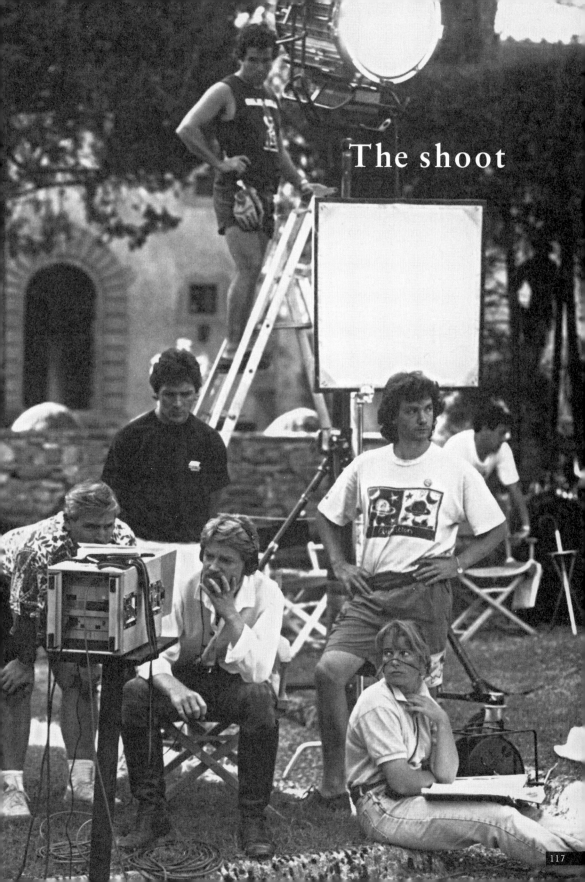

The shoot

Prize for most time-consuming moment. Scene one. Shot one.
Take 1. (No, make that a record-breaking take 29.) This move,
from a first full-frame view of the painting, ending up on a close-
up of Beatrice sitting in the tree, involved the perfect coordination
of sun, actors, camera track and zoom, cleavage, bare chests,
bread slicing, song lyrics, and donkey. It took a while.

How come we get horses called Tornado, Monster, Suicide Sal', and Meltdown?

Keep in a straight line! Look, can someone explain to Tornado the concept of straight?

Guaranteed hi-tech, non-horse-spooking tracking camera vehicle. Not entirely risk free for the operator.

Look, it's perfectly simple with animals. You have to think of Suicide Sal' as your friend.

(Sigh) OK, get me Meltdown on the radio. I'm going to talk him down.

Emma Thompson (left)
Tim Harvey (right)

Now look, Mr. Designer. This garden swing you've built for me to move very violently in will **work**, won't it?

Jimmy Yuill (left)
Pat Doyle (right)

Musicians and singers performing live. We insisted on this for each of the musical sequences, and so the nervous participants were found in corners everywhere, searching for the lost key.

Phyllis Dalton (left)
Kenneth Branagh (right)

Costume decisions hell. One hundred and twenty extras. One hundred costumes. Well, look. Strictly speaking, do we actually think Shakespeare intended all of them to be...fully clothed...as such...?

Russell Jackson (left)
Richard Briers (right)

Iambic instruction ill met by moonlight.

Denzel Washington (left)
Kenneth Branagh (right)

Intense discussions about just how hot it really is in
Tuscany in August. (104°)

Robert Sean Leonard (left)
Hugh Cruttwell (right)

The character demon and resident company truth
specialist homes in on Claudio.

High anxiety. Trouble brewing.

And here it is. We knew something was in the air. The famous Tuscan summer thunderstorm.

Now they tell us.

Producer agony as money is rained away.

Director on defensive:
'It's not my fault.'

Maybe the very sunny, funny gulling scene would **work** in the rain?

Instant guide to good filming weather
The producers are smiling again.

It's not possible to repeat this cameraman's
joke in a family publication.

Shakespeare's Hero.
One seriously cool gal.

Killing time between camera set-ups. The famous stone-plopped-in-goblet competition. Grand finale, USA v. U.K. (results to be announced).

Hi-tech heat-reduction systems on overdrive.

The good, the bad, and the nutty, in relaxation mode.

Get outa here! I'm telling you, **America** won that stone-plopped-in-goblet competition!

The advantage of having an acting double. He has to do all the wet things first.

Prize for most intense moment. Last scene. Last shot. Last take (19). Cue the music. Cue the exhausted Steadicam operator.

Remember, this is the last glorious shot. Be happy. Not sweaty. Eyes and teeth. Eyes and teeth.

But **don't** bump into the moving camera. It has to go right through the house following the delirious revellers into the courtyard.

Cue the confetti. Don't mess up the
lip-synch on the song lyrics.
Avoid falling into the courtyard well.

Cue the crane operator.
Stand by to take
cameraman ninety feet
into the air.

Cue the dancing in the back garden for the aerial
sequence. We can't **stop!** This shot lasts four
minutes. Don't mess up. Physical, heat-related,
dance-induced breakdowns not possible till the
crane reaches its full height and we yell cut.

Six months' planning, eight hours,
four minutes, nineteen takes, two
hundred sweating actors and
crew later, we think we have it.

Well done, team.

Right. Moving on. Next set-up!

The Unit Photograph.
The one thing that half the unit are always guaranteed to miss.
Arrivederci!

The Samuel Goldwyn Company presents
A Renaissance Films Production
of a Kenneth Branagh Film

MUCH ADO ABOUT NOTHING

by William Shakespeare
Adapted for the screen by Kenneth Branagh

Cast in order of appearance

Leonato	Richard Briers
Hero	Kate Beckinsale
Margaret	Imelda Staunton
Friar Francis	Jimmy Yuill
Antonio	Brian Blessed
George Seacole	Andy Hockley
Frances Seacole	Chris Barnes
Hugh Oatcake	Conrad Nelson
Ursula	Phyllida Law
Beatrice	Emma Thompson
Messenger	Alex Lowe
Don Pedro	Denzel Washington
Don John	Keanu Reeves
Conrade	Richard Clifford
Borachio	Gerard Horan
Claudio	Robert Sean Leonard
Benedick	Kenneth Branagh
Balthasar	Patrick Doyle
Dogberry	Michael Keaton
Verges	Ben Elton
Sexton	Edward Jewesbury

Costume Designer
Phyllis Dalton

Production Designer
Tim Harvey

Editor
Andrew Marcus

Director of Photography
Roger Lanser

Music by
Patrick Doyle

Produced by
Stephen Evans David Parfitt Kenneth Branagh

Directed by
Kenneth Branagh